MW00770205

Date Like You Know What You're Doing

Michael Johnson

Your DatePrep Guide

DATE LIKE YOU KNOW WHAT YOU'RE DOING
Your DatePrep Guide

The Holy Bible, English Standard Version. ESV® Text Edition: 2016.
Copyright © 2001 by Crossway Bibles, a publishing ministry of Good News Publishers.
New American Standard Bible®, Copyright © 1960, 1971, 1977, 1995, 2020
by The Lockman Foundation. All rights reserved.

ISBN 978-1-66787-138-7 (Print)
ISBN 978-1-66787-139-4 (eBook)

Designed by: BookBaby
Edited by: DragonflyWings.Ink, a division of Lori Lynn Enterprises

For permission requests, speaking inquiries, and bulk order purchase options,
email info@F-M-U.com.

Future Marriage University
188 Front Street Suite 116-17
Franklin, TN 37064

FMUniversity.net

With an encyclopedic breadth and deep-sea diving depth, Michael Johnson explores, unpacks, and presents the ins and outs of responsible dating. The vision of "a life-giving, lifelong marriage that blesses the world as much as it blesses the two of you" is inspiring, and the suggestions are as powerful as they are practical.

Though the writing style is fun, *Date Like You Know What You're Doing* is filled with enough "zinger" nuggets of wisdom to transform your thinking about how to date with God-honoring purpose and Jesus-loving Passion.

—**GARY THOMAS,** author of
Sacred Marriage and *The Sacred Search:
What If It's Not About Who You Marry, But Why?*

I loved this book! So many great truths, and written in a helpful, approachable voice. The best part of *Date Like You Know What You're Doing* is not only that it's insanely practical for scoping out and assessing potential dates and a future mate, but it's a great way to assess your own maturity and relationship potential. Unique, funny, biblical and comprehensive. Get this book and be willing to grow!

—**LISA ANDERSON,** author of
The Dating Manifesto and
host of "The Boundless Show"

MJ speaks right to the heart of what Christian dating should look like. He extracted and brought to life key Scriptures and practical principles in a humorous but no-nonsense fashion.

Date Like You Know What You're Doing is a comprehensive guide to smart dating every Christian should read, study, and follow.

—JOHN VAN EPP, Ph.D., author of
How to Avoid Falling in Love with a Jerk

Let's face it. Most people fumble and stumble their way through their dating years. Michael Johnson to the rescue. The insights and wisdom in this book can help you avoid some of the bruises and scars, and point you in the direction of a strong, healthy relationship.

—BOB LEPINE, author of
Love Like You Mean It and
Build a Stronger Marriage

MJ has been delivering reliable and unbiased instruction on the touchy topics of sex, dating, and relationships for almost 20 years. All of that vital information and accurate guidance truly shines in *Date Like You Know What You're Doing*.

If you want to date, read this book first. If you're already dating, read it before it's too late!

—JOE S. MCILHANEY, JR., M.D.,
Founder/CEO Medical Institute

Over the years that I have known MJ it has become clear to me that he has a passion and a calling to help young people find the pathway to lifelong marriage. He and I have discussed many times how vitally important a great marriage is in all of our lives to our overall success, and how little preparation is usually invested in marriage as compared to, say, getting a college degree. One gives you a job (which is also important) but the other gives you a good, and meaningful overall life.

At God's direction, MJ has invested his life into doing something about this paradoxical situation. He has learned a great deal along the way and he is graciously willing to share. I believe that young people who read *Date Like You Know What You Are Doing* will in fact know what they are doing by the time they are done, and will have made a monumentally important investment in one of life's most important and rewarding endeavors!

—**DR. JOE MALONE,** co-author of
*Battles of the Sexes: Raising Sexual IQ to Lower
Sexual Conflict and Empower Lasting Love*

Date Like You Know What You're Doing is fabulous!

So full of rich info, but it's "nugget size" so you can actually digest it; like it's already put into an application format. That's so much more enjoyable for the reader who actually has time to process AND apply. It's like MJ has already done the heavy lifting for you!

And of course, his humor and style trick you into thinking you're eating chips instead of vegetables! Like, "I'm having fun reading this, so how can this possibly be good for me?"

—**AMI SAUER,** mom of teenage sons

This is an extraordinary book. It has the prophetic edge of Amos and John the Baptist, but the style is disarming. It makes cold logic warm. It provides a nice balance, such as when Michael tempers gratifying talk of godly relationships—"the land of milk and honey" and the "balm of Gilead" if you will—with notes on the hard work involved in finding good pastureland, negotiating beehives, and dealing with flies in the ointment.

No, Michael's not writing inerrant, infallible scripture, but he aptly quotes and applies a lot of the Bible. And he serves up plenty of prudential wisdom of his own. The vast majority of it elicits a hearty "Amen!" some of it an "Oh, my!" and an occasional "Say what?!" But it all takes you places you need to go in your thinking.

It's a fascinating read, with granular, plain speaking, moved along briskly with entertaining prose, e.g., the "three-step process" for avoiding linkage with fools is "1. Take 2. Your 3. Time" and then the commandment, "Thou shalt not treat red flags like they are part of a carnival."

We've heard that singles should "kiss dating goodbye." Michael and Julie (his bride of nearly thirty years) urge rather that we should "kiss dumb dating goodbye."

Throughout, he's generously self-effacing and candid about his own missteps and struggles. For all this, we can be grateful that they make their case emphatically and persuasively—that scripture/reason/prayer-saturated dating is doable and urgent, for the glory of God and the blessing of all concerned.

—**MARK COPPENGER**, B.A., Ouachita;
M.A., Ph.D., Vanderbilt; M.Div., Southwestern;
and author of *If Christianity Is So Good,
Why Are Christians So Bad?*

Dedicated to
Holt, Claire, Bethany, Clive James, and Tim

CONTENTS

INTRODUCTION:

IS THIS BOOK FOR YOU?

I'll never forget when I was in my early 20s and my mom gave me a marriage book for Christmas. Not a dating book, like this one, but a *marriage* book. And I didn't even have a girlfriend!

"I get it, mom. You want grandkids."

Regardless, I read it over Christmas vacation, and within thirty days I was dating the woman I eventually married. And I'm really glad I did. (Both read that book and married that girl!)

But enough about me. How about you? Would you like to avoid heartbreak, rejection, and regret? Or beyond avoiding bad things, would you like to truly succeed in your dating life? And by "succeed," I don't just mean eventually get married, but do so with great memories to look back on and an amazing future to look forward to?

If you just answered that last question with a "Heck yeah," then this is the book for you.

Let's face it. Relationships are hard. And a dating relationship? It's like a long division problem you have to solve by hand. One wrong calculation and you're not coming up with the right answer. And discerning where you went wrong can be like trying to find a needle in a love shack … or love in a haystack … or whatever mixed metaphor you want to use.

SHOULD YOU READ THIS BOOK NOW?

In hindsight, I realize I was given an incredible opportunity that one Christmas. That was the moment I began preparing for the most important earthly relationship in my entire life. And since I read that book at a time when I didn't have love chemicals flooding my brain (inhibiting clear thinking), and I didn't have a relationship to defend (persuading me to ignore wise counsel), I actually internalized much of what that book had to offer. I drank in the wisdom as if I somehow knew it might come in handy.

And it did! Which is why after ten years of marriage, I sensed God asking me to go back and reread that book with the goal of figuring out how to trick other people into doing what my mom tricked me into doing. That led to the founding of our organization, Future Marriage University (FMU), and me writing this book for you.

Will you begin dating the person you'll end up marrying within thirty days of reading this book? Or are you already dating them? Or maybe you've met them, but haven't begun dating? Perhaps they're a friend you've known for years but have never seen in "that way." Or on the other hand, you may very much see them in "that way," but you've been friend-zoned. For now.

I don't know those answers. What I do know is that I'm praying for the day when ten years after your wedding you remember this book, and you praise God you read it now.

MY DATING LIFE BEFORE I READ THAT BOOK

Truth is, I didn't date at all in high school. It never comes as a shocker when I share this at live events, where people can see what I look like. In this one respect, I am incredibly Christlike, as Jesus had, "no beauty that we should desire him" (Isaiah 53:2b ESV).

But the reasons behind my high school datelessness weren't solely due to my appearance or my social awkwardness. I also held high standards. And not just about a girl's looks, but about her love for Jesus.

By my teens, I had already developed a relationship with God that was intensely real to me, and I had little interest in dating a girl who couldn't relate to my passion for Jesus. Sadly for me, St. Louis, where I grew up, wasn't the proverbial buckle of the metaphorical Bible belt. So in the end, there were only two girls I mustered up the courage to ask out in high school. And they both said, "No."

They actually said, "I'd really rather just be friends." And one of them told me that three different times—in one phone call.

That said, a major paradigm shift took place when I left for college. A Christian college. Suddenly my dating prospects changed for the better. Like for the really, really better.

It was as if the scales fell from my eyes, and I looked and I saw that it was good: gorgeous, godly girls everywhere! In fact, I went out with more than 30 different college coeds my freshman year alone.

You may not believe that number. I don't know that I would believe it if I were you, but three words simply explain how a guy like me could go out with over 30 different girls in one school year: favorable gender ratio. In other words, I was practically the only date option for many of the girls I dated. There simply weren't many men asking.

You might think, "Bummer for them," but I was a fun date. I could be funny too, and I liked to be creative. In fact, my dating life included a red convertible Cadillac with a car phone (before there were cell phones), a private plane flight, a secret agent adventure across campus videoed live (back when video cameras sat on your shoulder instead of in your pocket), a candlelit dinner at McDonald's, and a moonlit picnic on the 50-yard line of my college stadium (until gunmen ran us out).

So, what's your dating story? Are you waiting for your dating life to begin? Are you enjoying the time of your dating life? Are you dating, but hating it? Or have you sworn off dating altogether?

THE PURPOSE OF THIS BOOK

Wherever you are in your journey, I'd like to empower you to grow spiritually and date wisely so you can marry well.

To accomplish that end, this book offers you love education. We call it LoveEd for short and it's the missing link between the sex education kids get when they're young and the premarital counseling couples only get after they believe they've already found "the one."

And don't be frightened by the "M-word." *Marriage!* Fear not! Unlike the book my mom gave me, this is a *dating* book, not a marriage book. However, as with any successful endeavor, you have to begin with the end in mind. The ultimate goal, if you will.

So what do you want to be the ultimate goal of your dating life?

- Just dating?
- Just getting a significant other?
- Just making out?
- Just moving from dating partner to dating partner?
- Just moving in together?
- Just getting engaged?
- Just making it to the wedding day?

How about this ultimate goal: a life-giving, lifelong marriage that blesses the world as much as it blesses the two of you. If that's a mission you can accept and get excited about, then you want to keep reading!

Even cooler, as you discover how relationships work and how they don't, you will learn how to avoid as much heartbreak, rejection, and regret as humanly possible.

DON'T JUST FOLLOW THESE PRINCIPLES

All of that to say, it's not my intention with this book to define exactly how Christians are supposed to date. There are clear truths—crystal clear truths—I will share from scripture that you should treat as the gospel truth because they are drawn from God's Word. But the rest of the words are mine.

So, on the one hand, don't approach this study as if it's going to give you all the perfect answers and remove every opportunity for failure. It is only a guide. I don't know everything. I certainly don't know you and the intricacies of your relational gifts and challenges.

On the other hand, I urge you to not discount everything you don't like in this book. Wisdom is often unpleasant and discipline often unwelcome. However, in addition to drawing many truths from scripture, there is something to be said for spending 18+ years studying the topics of sex, dating, and relationships. And something else to be said from looking at these topics from the perspective of 29 years of marriage and 25 years of parenting.

All of that said, I don't want you to just follow a set of principles. I want you to follow a *person*: Jesus Christ.

So, are you in? Then let's do this thing! But first, two more suggestions for getting the most out of this book.

PASS ON WHAT YOU HAVE LEARNED!

I urge you to share with other wise individuals what makes sense to you in these pages because LoveEd is for sharing. So I pray you will help those you care about, *not* judge them in your heart or talk about them behind their backs.

No one needs the Dating Police or the Courtship Gestapo, but everyone needs a good friend who wants the very best for them and desires it enough to tell them when they may be making mistakes they will regret their entire lives.

In the end, I hope you'll dig into this book with the intention not only of changing your own dating life but also changing the dating lives of those you care about.

EVERYTHING'S BETTER WITH FRIENDS

Speaking of your friends, all of the content of this book came out of an 8-week LoveEd class I've taught for years, and so I encourage you to get some friends together and go through this book as a group study. Here's the chapter breakdown for those 8 weeks:

- Week 1: Intro & Chapter 1
- Week 2: Chapters 2 & 3
- Week 3: Chapters 4–6
- Week 4: Chapters 7–10
- Week 5: Chapters 11–14
- Week 6: Chapters 15–17
- Week 7: Chapters 18–20
- Week 8: Chapter 21

Simply read the appropriate chapters for each week and discuss. To take your study to the next level, you'll find a link at the end of each section of the book to unlock and access exclusive content including group study questions and applicable videos and blog posts.

CHAPTER 1:
DO YOU HAVE A LICENSE TO DATE?

Our culture tends to approach dating a lot like learning to ride a bike. It's a rite of passage. It's part of growing up. And frankly, if you ever want to learn, you have to just get out there and try it.

Scrapes and bruises are considered normal and are expected to heal in time. And if you fall? You get back up and try again.

Actually, in practice, dating is treated even more casually than learning to ride a bike. After all, any parent letting little Bobby mount a bicycle without a helmet today could have a team of child service agents swarm in with a sting operation within minutes.

In contrast, with dating there is nothing like a helmet to guard your head, nothing like training wheels to keep you steady, and no one with you or even watching you in case you fall. The way dating is practiced in our culture, you're sent on your way with almost no instruction, completely on your own, and largely unprotected. Does this sound like a winning plan for dating success?

THE COLD HARD REALITY OF DATING

To be accurate, dating is far more like learning to drive a car than learning to ride a bike.

It *is* a rite of passage, but it is also dangerous because you're not merely risking your knees and elbows when you fall. Instead, when you're dating, you're putting your heart out there to potentially be bruised and battered. Many feel negative dating experiences leave their heart feeling "totaled."

In addition to greater danger, there's greater difficulty. Far from a bike ride in the park, negotiating a dating relationship can be as complicated as navigating rush hour traffic on an eight-lane highway. Blindfolded.

In short, like learning to drive a car, dating is both a dangerous and complicated endeavor. That's why it's not so easy to just get back up again after you fall out of love (or someone falls out of love with you). A broken heart isn't equivalent to a skinned knee. It takes more than a Band-aid.

So in a way, you could say you ought to have to obtain a license before you date. But you don't. You just jump behind the wheel and start driving. However, dating without a license (i.e., without any training or understanding of what you're doing) is directionless at best and dangerous at worst.

DO YOU KNOW WHERE YOU WANT YOUR DATING LIFE TO TAKE YOU?

Think back in time to your last family road trip with the parental units. I'm going to guess your parents (and maybe even you) knew the following before you ever left town:

- Where you were going
- How you were going to get there
- Where you were going to stay
- What you might do while you were there
- How your vacation would be funded

In light of that, let me ask you this: "When it comes to dating, do you know where you're going?"

> *For which one of you, when he wants to build a tower, does not first sit down and calculate the cost to see if he has enough to complete it? Otherwise, when he has laid a foundation and is not able to finish, all who observe it begin to ridicule him, saying, 'This man began to build and was not able to finish.' Or what king, when he sets out to meet another king in battle, will not first sit down and consider whether he is strong enough with ten thousand men to encounter the one coming against him with twenty thousand? Or else, while the other is still far away, he sends a delegation and asks for terms of peace.* —Luke 14:28-32 NASB

Isn't your future marriage a bigger deal than a family road trip? Don't you want to build something through your dating life that you can complete, and which will stand the test of time? Isn't it as important for you to succeed in marriage as it would be for a king to succeed in war?

If so, then where would you like your dating life to take you?

- Into a relationship with a significant other?
- Into a relationship with a "roommate with benefits"?
- All the way to marriage? Any marriage? What kind of marriage?

Don't date directionless! If you want a successful dating life, you have to know where you want your dating life to take you.

WHAT'S REALLY AT STAKE WHEN YOU DATE?

According to scripture, King Solomon was the wisest man to ever live (other than the God-man, Jesus).

God gave Solomon a once-in-a-lifetime genie-in-a-bottle offer: "Ask whatever you wish."

And Solomon answered, "Wisdom, please."

And God said (loosely translated), "You got it, Solo. And because I'm so pleased with your request, I'm giving you wealth and fame to go with it."

But do you know what happened to Solomon in his later years?

> *Now King Solomon loved many foreign women, along with the daughter of Pharaoh: Moabite, Ammonite, Edomite, Sidonian, and Hittite women, from the nations concerning which the Lord had said to the people of Israel, "You shall not enter into marriage with them, neither shall they with you, for surely **they will turn away your heart** after their gods." Solomon clung to these in love. He had 700 wives, who were princesses, and 300 concubines. And **his wives turned away his heart**. For when Solomon was old **his wives turned away his heart** after other gods, and his **heart** was not wholly true to the Lord his God, as was the **heart** of David his father.* —1 King 11:1-4 ESV (emphasis mine)

The "heart" is mentioned five times in these four verses, with three of those references revealing how the women whom Solomon loved "turned his heart away" from the Lord. According to *Strong's Concordance*, the Hebrew word for "heart" in this passage has a broad meaning encompassing the "inner man, mind, will, heart, soul, understanding."[1]

Have you thought about how precious your heart is? As your blood-pumping organ is essential to life, so your metaphorical heart is the central core of who you are:

- Your feelings (including all your hopes and fears, joys and regrets)
- Your will (including all your desires and convictions)
- Your intellect (including all your thoughts and questions)

---

[1] "H3824 - Lēḇāḇ - Strong's Hebrew Lexicon (KJV)," Blue Letter Bible, accessed May 28, 2022, https://www.blueletterbible.org/lexicon/h3824/kjv/wlc/0-1/.

Your heart—that is what you risk every time you date. Even when you're thinking, *What the hay. I'll just give this person a chance.* No one can predict when they will fall in love. No one.

Do you think risking your heart is a small thing? Apparently, the wisest man in the world once thought the same. However, true to God's warning, when Solomon chose to give his heart to women who did not follow the God of scriptures, bad things happened. Really bad things. And not just for Solomon, but for the entire nation of Israel.

Think you have your heart in hand? You can't forget you also risk the heart of everyone you date as well. Aren't their hearts as precious as yours? Then let me encourage you to date accordingly.

WHAT IT MEANS TO "GUARD YOUR HEART"

Bottom line, your heart is a treasure to God. Far more precious than it ever will be to anyone you date or marry because God is our Creator who formed your heart, knows your heart, and died (literally) to win your heart for your good and His glory. This is why God commands us in Proverbs 4:23 to guard our heart.

Above all else, guard your heart, for everything you do flows from it.

This passage is commonly interpreted to mean God doesn't want us to risk wounding our heart. And following this line of thinking, many avoid dating seriously or even dating at all, while others wait for supernatural signs or words from God they believe will keep them from ever getting hurt in the dating process.

However, trying to protect your heart from all hurt is not only the wrong goal, it's an unfeasible goal for anyone who sets out to love like Jesus. As C.S. Lewis states so clearly in *The Four Loves* …

"To love at all is to be vulnerable. Love anything and your heart will be wrung and possibly broken. If you want to make sure of keeping it intact you must give it to no one, not even an animal. Wrap it carefully round with hobbies and little luxuries; avoid all entanglements. Lock it up safe in the casket or coffin of your selfishness. But in that casket, safe, dark, motionless, airless, it will change. It will not be broken; it will become unbreakable, impenetrable, irredeemable. To love is to be vulnerable."[2]

Instead of trying to protect your heart from hurt, the writer of Proverbs is encouraging us to protect our heart from *needless* hurt; the kind of hurt we invite on ourselves by living foolishly. The kind of hurt King Solomon endured. Consider the three verses which precede verse 23 in Proverbs 4:

My son, pay attention to what I say; turn your ear to my words.
Do not let them out of your sight, keep them within your heart;
for they are life to those who find them and health to one's
whole body. (NIV)

The goal is not to avoid vulnerability but stupidity. Bottom line: If you want a successful dating life, you must learn how to wisely guard your own heart, as well as the hearts of those you date. We accomplish this by keeping our hearts in the hands of our God, even while we seek His will in risking our heart by loving others, particularly by loving someone enough to enter an exclusive dating relationship.

AN ANALOGY FOR WHY RELATIONSHIPS ARE SO COMPLICATED

Imagine I wanted to paint a picture of a lemming.

Perhaps that doesn't sound like an impossibility to you. Perhaps you're an accomplished painter and have always raised lemmings as pets. In that

---

[2] "Bookquoters," 30+ quotes from *The Four Loves* by C.S. Lewis, accessed May 28, 2022, https://bookquoters.com/book/the-four-loves.

case, you could paint a lemming with your eyes closed. With no drop cloth. However, there are some parameters you should know about me as I approach this artistic endeavor.

First, let's assume I don't even know what a lemming looks like because I've never seen one, but I've heard they resemble something like a cross between a guinea pig and a wolverine.

Secondly, I don't know how to paint, but I'm pretty sure I can do it because I've seen it done on TV. And by "seen it done on TV," I don't mean I've watched Bob Ross instructional videos. I mean to say I've seen shows and movies where painting was being done as part of the action on screen. (I can remember the movies *Emma* and *Little Women* in particular. And I've watched them more than once.) All of that to say, I have no training, but it doesn't look that hard. You just put the brush in the paint and then put the paint on the paper. Or canvas. Or wood. (I believe the Mona Lisa was painted on a wood panel and I have some plywood in the garage.)

Thirdly, I don't want to take the time to get paintbrushes, so I thought I'd just use a hairbrush. (A brush is a brush, right?)

Lastly, before I start, I'm going to drink a little alcohol. Or maybe a lot. Just enough to feel more relaxed. And artistic.

Now, what is my painting going to look like?

Someone *might* mistake it for modern art, but no one's going to look at my painting and say, "Oh what a lovely lemming! It almost looks like a photograph."

Now here's the analogy …

For starters, most unmarried people in our world today, hoping to carry on a life-giving romance, have likely never observed one single healthy dating relationship in the course of their natural lives. It's an "animal" they've never laid eyes on.

However, they've seen how it's done in film, television, and videos. Not instructional videos, but they've watched infinitely more love scenes than I've watched painting scenes. And all that familiarity builds a level of confidence that overshadows my confidence in painting.

On top of this, most teens and young adults (or older adults, for that matter) have never acquired the right tools to thrive in a long-term, committed relationship. They only know how to sustain semi-intimate friendships and work relationships, and they've never felt that close to their family. So, they're like me in front of a scrap of plywood with tempera paint and a hairbrush.

Lastly, though many do engage in recreational drinking while dating (to feel more relaxed and sexy), you don't have to drink *anything* to have your judgment and sense of restraint seriously impaired by the neurochemistry of infatuation. (More on that in Chapters 12 and 20.) This is one of the reasons we enjoy being in love. It feels. So. Good!

So, the next time a friend asks you, "Why does dating have to be so complicated?" ask them if they've ever painted a picture of a lemming with a hairbrush. While drunk.

LOVE IS NOT ROCKET SCIENCE, BUT IT'S NOT MAGIC EITHER

"So what," you might say. "Romance is messy. It's love, not rocket science." But is that good enough for you? Is that what you want? An endless stream of complicated relationships? Hoping one of them will make it all the way to the altar? (Do you know the chances of an imprudent marriage ending in a painful divorce?)

Of course, from my research, most students and young adults don't want to be bothered thinking about engagement, marriage, and divorce when they're just trying to get a girlfriend or boyfriend. I get that. But while I don't want you to date out of fear of where things might end up, I do want you to understand the law of the harvest:

> *Do not be deceived, God is not mocked; for whatever a man sows, this he will also reap. For the one who sows to his own flesh will from the flesh reap corruption, but the one who sows to the Spirit will from the Spirit reap eternal life.* —Gal 6:7-8 NASB

You don't have to be a farmer to understand you can't plant cucumbers hoping to harvest tomatoes. If you want tomatoes, you have to plant tomatoes. If you want cucumbers, you have to plant cucumbers. And you're not going to get either if you're planting weeds.

However, when it comes to relationships, we often don't see the connection between the kinds of relational patterns we establish early in our dating life (and even before then) and the sort of marriage we wind up in.

We think we can be careless when we're dating, following our impulses and avoiding accountability (or even wise counsel). Then we can shape up when we get serious about marriage. But the Bible (like any farmer) tells us we will reap what we sow. And, as a friend I know likes to add, "Usually much later. And much more."

You simply cannot expect to wing it in your dating life, with no plan and no prudence, and then magically end up in a life-giving, lifelong marriage. God *is* gracious! But one of the ways God shows us His grace is by giving us His law and wisdom, along with qualities like self-control, so we can avoid the pitfalls of foolishness.

TWO WAYS WE REAP WHAT WE SOW

Let me be clear. God is *not* some mean, calculating boss who's chomping at the bit to write you up for every infraction just because He can. Or because He enjoys it.

That's often how we view God when we suffer for our choices, but it's neither a helpful nor complete way to look at life. God is a good Father who disciplines His children for their *good*, not His vindictive delight (see Hebrews 12).

However, in addition to God's disciplinary intervention, God established the world from the beginning so that those who live by wisdom generally enjoy good results from doing so—eventually. While those who reject wisdom generally incur negative results from doing so—eventually.

So, think of God's discipline less as a spanking for every time you cross the street without looking both ways and more as the natural result of getting hit by a car because you tried to cross the street without looking both ways.

That said, there are two main ways we wind up reaping what we sow:

- Choices we sow now reaping consequences later
- Choices we sow now reaping character later

To help us understand both of these ways of reaping what we sow, consider the results of our sexual choices.

HOW EACH SEXUAL EXPERIENCE CHANGES YOU

Common reasons for postponing sex until after marriage include the risk of unwanted pregnancy or sexually transmitted infections (STIs). This would be an example of sowing choices now that reap consequences later.

But let's say you have sex with several people before you marry, yet due to contraception and luck (because even the pill isn't 100% effective) no one becomes pregnant or gets any STIs.

Does that mean you escaped "judgment?" How could those choices still impact your marriage? Why can't you just wipe the anxious sweat off your then-married brow and enjoy the marriage bed?

Because every choice we make molds our character.

Every time we resist temptation, we become more and more the sort of person who can resist temptation. Conversely, every time we give into temptation, we become less and less the sort of person who can resist temptation. This is as true of sexual temptation as it is yielding to (or resisting) the temptation to eat junk food, shirk responsibilities, or tell lies.

So you may think, "I'm going to experiment sexually before marriage, but not after marriage. At least not with other people." But after experimenting sexually with half a dozen partners before marriage, is it even logical to think that, once you're married, you'll be perfectly content with just one partner for life, never to be tempted by another?

Can you see how naïve that thinking is? You might imagine that sex with the right partner will be so amazing you simply won't be able to imagine better sex with anyone else, but the reality is that variety invites comparison, and comparison invites discontentment.

Do some people manage to live a sexually promiscuous single life and then learn to rein in their sex drive in marriage? Yes! But it's far more difficult to break bad habits than it is to never establish them in the first place.

Relational patterns can be even more difficult to break. And we form relational patterns early. This next story is a sad example of this reality.

A YOUTH GROUP LOVE STORY GONE WRONG

I had been meeting with this friend of mine for some time as he struggled in his marriage. During one particular meeting over coffee, he shared with me that his wife was expecting. And he was not the father.

I was shocked! I mean, obviously, they were having issues. I knew that. But an affair? That resulted in a pregnancy! That's another level. Furthermore, this couple had met, fallen in love, and married in the same church. They were both believers and not only had children of their own but adopted more. The husband even worked in ministry.

How did this happen?

Well, there was more to the story, a part my friend never shared until after the revelation of his wife's affair. Only then did he divulge that when they were dating in school they would go through this cycle where she would cheat on him, then he would catch her, and then they would make up. And then he would cheat on *her*, and then she would catch *him*, and then they would make up. This little cycle was part of what kept the relationship interesting and exciting.

Crazy right? Maybe, but you must believe me, this was a model couple in our church. They were believers like you and me. Not perfect, but sincere and desiring a marriage that honored the Lord.

But they wound up reaping what they sowed. Their pattern of unfaithfulness in dating reaped unfaithfulness in marriage. And it was heartbreaking for both of them, as well as all their kids.

But the "cheat-get caught-make up" cycle finally ended. In divorce.

IT'S GOING TO TAKE MORE THAN A BOOK!

Just like learning to drive, you aren't going to learn everything by reading. You need one or more instructors. I'm talking about a mentor or two who are more experienced than you in life and relationships. Even better, find a married couple who enjoy the kind of marriage you would like to enjoy yourself.

Finally, I encourage you to invite other family and friends into your dating life and decisions. Not as literal chaperones accompanying you on every date, but as virtual passengers you invite into your dating process.

Why? Because of the existence of blind spots. Just like with driving a car, when it comes to any relationship, you can't see everything going on. This is especially true when your "vision" is impaired by the chemistry of romance.

It's nothing to be ashamed of. Everyone has blind spots, and no one can see them. If they could, they wouldn't be called "blind spots." So, if you want to maximize this time in your life and grow the best grand-slam relationships you can, then don't date alone. Begin by sharing with someone something you learned in this lesson.

This chapter marks the end of the first lesson in an 8-week LoveEd study. For discussion questions and resources go to:

FMUniversity.net/DatePrep-wk1

CHAPTER 2:

FRIENDS DON'T LET FRIENDS DATE DUMB

Truth is, I merely survived the dating process. I emerged with an amazing wife who, after 28+ years, is still my best friend. However, I made many missteps—ridiculous missteps—I never would have made had I examined and understood the motives which drove me to date in the first place.

Sadly, I'm not alone because poor motives for dating abound and often masquerade as harmless, reasonable, and even prudent.

COUNTDOWN: THE TOP 10 DUMBEST REASONS TO DATE

When you're looking at your motives, you're addressing the "why" question, which is the most important question you can answer about any life endeavor. And since poor dating motives are both so common and catastrophic, we're going to count down the TOP 10 dumbest reasons to date.

Some of these reasons many would readily claim. Others are common intentions few will admit to. Still, others are motivations hidden even from the ones driven by them. A few of the reasons are *not* inherently *wrong*, but they *are* insufficient. They can be a legitimate reason to date, but they cannot be the real driving force of your dating life, at least not if you wish to date in a healthy and whole way.

So, let's get to it! Let's answer that "why" question and root out what's really driving you to date.

DUMB REASON #10: BECAUSE I CAN

It's common for middle schoolers to wait until they reach a certain age before they date. Not by choice, of course, but "because their parents said so." So they wait until they're 13 or 16 or 18 or 80 until their parents say they can date.

Others wait until they leave their parents' home (and control) to start dating.

In many ways, I started dating just because I could. That is, when I could finally get a girl I was interested in to agree to a date.

However, if you started dating just because you could, I'm going to encourage you to *stop* dating until you come up with a better reason because license and freedom are not the same things.

> *All things are permitted for me, but not all things are of benefit. All things are permitted for me, but I will not be mastered by anything.*
> —1 Cor 6:12 NASB

Recognize Satan's Deception

More than being free to do what's within your rights, I want you to be free to do what's in your best interest. And in the end, that's part of the purpose of God's law: His greatest glory and your greatest good.

In contrast, Satan wants you to believe the purpose of God's law is to control you, but two truths expose this deception.

First truth: The God of the Bible is the sovereign Creator and Ruler of the universe.

If God wanted to control you, He would. Without any rules. And with both hands tied behind His back. He is that powerful.

Far from setting out to limit our freedom, God gives us His law to preserve our freedom.

Second truth: It is not the law that controls us or masters us, it is sin.

The law is always a choice: Obey or disobey and reap the corresponding consequences. But part of the consequences sin brings about is the reduced capacity to resist sin.

If you didn't notice, when the first temptation was given into, it was only forbidden fruit. But it escalated to murder in one generation. So who's the one looking to control us? It's not God with His law, but Satan with his deception. He knows the more we give in to sin, the more we are his, the less we are free, and the further we drift from who we were made to be.

The Right Question to Ask Before Dating (Or Anything)

If you could make any choice, why would you want to make the choice that threatens your freedom? Why would you choose immediate gratification over long-term blessing?

Well, because immediate gratification is so. Ah. Immediate. And gratifying.

But it's also fleeting. And oftentimes rather disappointing.

Many who date, just because they can, find this to be true. So the right question is never, "Can you," but, "Should you?"

DUMB REASON #9: EVERYONE IS DOING IT

Do you want to date because all your friends seem to be? Or perhaps because all your friends who are dating seem so happy?

Though I can't speak to your social circle, I can tell you this. Statistically across the nation, not only is everyone *not* dating or in a serious relationship, *most* are not dating or in a serious relationship.

Do You Sense God Calling You to Blend In?

Even if everyone *were* dating or in a serious relationship, what would be your motive for following the crowd? It's an important question to consider when we observe that God seldom calls His people to blend in.

- He called Noah to build a zoo. A really big zoo. Which could float. But not near the water. At first.

- He called Moses to tell the ruler of Egypt to set all the Hebrew slaves in his nation free. For free. Through the use of a few miraculous signs which soon got the attention of the entire nation.

- He called Joshua to assault a city with a marching band armed only with horns. They didn't even have drums.

- Then He called the entire nation of Israel not to blend in, but to intentionally stand apart from the other nations around them.

Finally, He says this to those who are His followers, both back then and today:

> *You are the light of the world. A city set on a hill cannot be hidden. Nor do people light a lamp and put it under a basket, but on a stand, and it gives light to all in the house. In the same way, let your light shine before others, so that they may see your good works and give glory to your Father who is in heaven.* —Matt 5:14-16 ESV

Are you dating (or do you want to date) because everyone's doing it? Consider how that's working out for everyone.

DUMB REASON #8: JUST FOR FUN

There's nothing wrong with having fun on a date. We believe dating can (and should) be a *lot* of fun.

However, the keyword in this dumb reason is the word "just," as in that's all there is to one's dating aspirations. And that's "just" not good enough, because if dating is the chosen method of mate selection for our culture (which for better or worse it is), then there ought to be a little gravity associated with it.

Most of us know this, so the reality is many who claim to be dating "just for fun" are using that explanation as a cover for other more serious (or desperate or dark) motivations which drive them, either consciously or subconsciously.

Is Dating About the Experience or the Relationship?

To be sure, fun was a huge motive for my dating life back in college. And I wanted my date to have as much fun as I did. Maybe even more fun, the way an actor wants their audience to enjoy the show.

To that end, like a good entertainer, I tried to be creative and keep everything light. I wanted a date with me to be memorable—more of an experience than just dinner and a movie. But while I was striving to give my dates a fun time, I was missing something.

Should I have planned every detail of every date with the goal of "wowing" my date (or even the more modest goal of giving her a good time), or should I have simply set out to get to know her?

Would my dating life have been more enjoyable had I succeeded in entertaining every girl I took out? Or would it have been more enjoyable had I succeeded in getting to know every girl I took out?

I see now that I spent most of my dating life chasing experiences, instead of building relationships.

Do You Know Jesus or Have You Only Experienced Him?

The crowds all got to experience Jesus. They got to be there when He turned water to wine; fed thousands with a little basket of fish and chips; cast out demons; healed the blind, lame, leprous, sick; and brought the occasional dead person back to life.

No doubt that was all amazing fun to experience, to actually be there and then tell others the stories as long as you lived. But the disciples, and the women Jesus was close to, got to know Him—His character, perspective, and personality. And it changed them in a way those who merely experienced Jesus could never understand, even long after Jesus' death, resurrection, and ascension.

Consider Peter and John when they were brought before Jewish leaders after healing a lame man (in Acts 4). You would think a miracle like that would warrant a little shock and awe, but they seemed more annoyed. However, we read this:

> *Now when they saw the boldness of Peter and John and perceived*
> *that they were uneducated, common men, they were astonished.*
> *And they recognized that they had been with Jesus.* —Acts 4:13 ESV

What astonished them was not the healing power possessed by Peter and John, but the confidence they possessed. "And they recognized that they had been with Jesus."

How cool would it be if everyone you dated wasn't so much impressed by your party tricks as they were impacted by the personality—the courage, kindness, and patience—Jesus has wrought in you over years of being in relationship with him? How would that change the way you approached dating?

Is Dating Ever Really Just for Fun?

If I had been more honest back in the day, dating was never just for fun for me. It was always more than that because I desperately longed for a girlfriend.

I didn't want to entertain a different "audience" night after night, content to enjoy the applause as the curtain dropped. I hoped that eventually one of those girls would want an encore performance, and keep coming back for more. And that instead of applause, I might get a kiss at the end of the evening.

I know I'm not the only one who's pretended to date "just for fun" when I was really trying to meet deeper needs. How about you?

DUMB REASON #7: SOMEBODY ASKED ME

Should you accept any date invitation? Or should you ask someone out just because you know they're into you? Consider the following questions:

- Are they really into you, but you only think of them like a cousin?

- Are they really looking for a significant other and hope to confirm that relationship status on a first date?

- Are they actually hoping for marriage and would like to book the venue on the first date?

- Do they just want to hook up? And what kind of hook up?

- Do *you* just want to hook up? And what kind of hook up?

In other words, is it fair to ask for some transparency when it comes to dating?

Truth Is the Lifeblood of Healthy Relationships

In retrospect, I've decided the two young ladies who turned down my first date invitations back in high school did me a favor. They let me know where I stood with them. Clearly. Which, when it came to romantic possibilities, was nowhere. But at least I knew the truth.

Yet when it comes to dating, truth is often in short supply.

This is tragic because truth is the lifeblood of healthy relationships, yet it's rare for a young man and woman to share a clear understanding of what they expect from a first date. And even rarer for a couple to maintain an accurate picture of where their relationship is in the present and where it might be headed.

How to Learn to Tell the Truth

So how do we fix this? Is there a magic strategy for walking the line between endless uncertainty and impulsive declarations of emotion? How do you balance the desire to protect yourself with the desire to express yourself?

How do you learn to tell the truth in your dating life in a healthy way?

By learning to tell the truth in less complicated relationships with family and friends. But we often don't. Instead, we learn to present ourselves to parents, siblings, church friends, school friends, and the rest of the world in whatever ways are most likely to elicit a positive reaction in each particular relationship.

Then we run off and date the same way.

In other words, if you can't be honest and vulnerable with the people who know you best and love you most, how can you expect to do that in dating?

You can't. You will either learn to hide your feelings or let them lead you to say anything. Or you might even bounce between the two extremes.

This is why I urge you to intentionally seek to grow in relational intimacy with good, same-gender friendships before you consider dating. Can you get hurt by friends? Sure, but unmet expectations and unrequited affection are far more common in romance.

> Better is open rebuke than hidden love. Faithful are the wounds of a friend; profuse are the kisses of an enemy. —Prov 27:5-6 ESV

Many a dater have wound up kissing someone they now consider an enemy. Some have kissed many enemies. Or worse. So take care before you accept or extend that date invite. First seek the wise counsel of a faithful friend.

DUMB REASON #6: I'M CURIOUS

At age nine, I was dying to have a girlfriend, curious to know how it felt to fall in love, and (more importantly) to have someone fall in love with me.

When it comes to love and romance, what are *you* curious about? Curiosity is healthy, but we have to be wise in where we go to satisfy our curiosity. For instance, it's normal for a young child to be curious about the physical anatomy of the opposite sex, but far better for that child to ask a trusted adult than to go to the internet and search for "naked …."

Are you curious about sex? Do you wonder what boundaries you should set or how you can keep from going too far?

Are you curious about romance? Do you wonder what the difference is between true love and infatuation, or how you can tell if someone likes you?

Are you curious about dating? Do you wonder if you should ask someone out or how to just be yourself on a date?

All those questions are fabulous! But don't turn your dating life into a social science experiment where you play with the brain chemistry of romance.

Something's likely to blow up in your face.

Instead, seek answers *before* dating from mentors and books. These resources will not only help you discover the answers you're looking for but will also help you understand yourself, which is essential for healthy dating.

> *The purpose in a man's heart is like deep water, but a man of understanding will draw it out. Many a man proclaims his own steadfast love, but a faithful man who can find?* —Prov 20:5-6 ESV

Curiosity is a marvelous part of a healthy dating life, but your curiosity should be directed toward getting to know everything you can about the people you date, not wondering how this whole dating thing works.

Dating, like any adventure, will be a learning experience, but the adventure of dating isn't an undertaking for people who have no idea what they're doing. After all, dating is like learning to drive a car. Remember?

God Cares About *Why* You Date More Than *Who*

Here's a little-known secret to understanding God's will: God is far less concerned with what we do than He is with *why* we do what we do.

Does God not care about obedience? Certainly! But what is your heart attitude behind your obedience?

- Do you obey God out of love or duty?
- Do you obey God to honor Him or keep Him off your back?
- Do you obey God because you trust His goodness or fear His retribution?

Bottom line, obeying matters, but why we obey matters more. Who you date and how you date matters, but if you have the right reasons for dating—the right "why" for your dating life—you will be less likely to date those you shouldn't or date in ways you shouldn't. Keep that in mind as you reflect on the previous five dumb reasons for dating, and as we hit the Top 5 in our next chapter.

CHAPTER 3:
TOP 5 DUMBEST REASONS TO DATE

Our motives are directly tied to the questions we want our dating life to answer.

- Am I attractive?
- Am I normal?
- Am I special?
- Am I accepted?
- Am I interesting?
- Am I funny?
- Am I fun?
- Am I desirable?

All of those questions are common, but they are also weighty because they are related to how we perceive ourselves. They have to do with our identity.

That said, when you look for the wrong things from your relationships, or even when you look for the *right* things from the *wrong* relationships, you risk not getting your questions answered. Or worse, you may get the *wrong* answers.

- I'm *not* attractive … or … I'm attractive
  only if I dress provocatively.

- I'm *not* normal … or … I'm normal
  if I lower my standards.

- I'm *not* special … or … I'm special
  if I can keep a significant other.

- I'm *not* accepted … or … I'm accepted
  if I will give into sexual advances.

- I'm *not* interesting … or … I'm interesting
  when I gossip about others.

- I'm *not* funny … or … I'm funny
  when I am crass or profane.

- I'm *not* fun … or … I'm fun when I'm drinking.

- I'm *not* desirable … or … I'm desirable
  if the other person is drinking.

In the end, if you keep dating for dumb reasons, you're going to hurt some-one. Probably "someones." And one of those "someones" is likely to be you. So in the interest of less heartbreak, rejection, and regret, let's finish off our countdown of wrong motives with the Top 5 Dumbest Reasons to Date.

DUMB REASON #5: STATUS

Is dating important to your status? What kind of status are you looking for?

- Getting a certain person to go out with you?
- Getting a lot of people to go out with you?
- Just getting *anyone* to go out with you?

This was definitely an influence on my desire to date, but today, in the era of social media where status is everything, it cranks this motivation up to an 11. However, you cannot care about people and status at the same time.

Compare the desire for status to Paul's admonition:

> *Have this mind among yourselves, which is yours in Christ Jesus, who, though he was in the form of God, did not count equality with God a thing to be grasped, but emptied himself, by taking the form of a servant, being born in the likeness of men. And being found in human form, he humbled himself by becoming obedient to the point of death, even death on a cross.* —Phil 2:5-8 ESV

At the end of the day, if I'm dating to attain a certain status, I'm using people, and using people doesn't build relationships. It may build your status—temporarily. But your character will suffer.

DUMB REASON #4: BELONGING

It is natural, it is normal, it is healthy, and it is human to want to belong.

Our Creator designed human physiology such that we require almost two decades of nurturing before we are ready to live on our own. No other species in the animal kingdom requires such a long maturation process.

In an ideal world, all those years of childrearing should enable us to grow up *knowing* we belong from the start to a family.

But things don't always work out like that, do they?

Many of us feel as distant from our parents as we do from the moon. Maybe this is due to our parents' failure to nurture us. Maybe this is due to our failure to submit to their nurturing. Probably some of both. Regardless, we were made to belong, and so we seek to belong.

For many, this is the driving force of their dating desires. It was for me.

I desperately. Wanted. To belong. To someone!

I wanted to be chosen!

The Secret to Belonging

Now logic would tell you that people who are alone feel alone and people who are not alone do not.

Curiously, feelings often defy logic, which leads us to a truth that's taken me decades to grasp: Belonging is something you only feel when you believe it.

Some folks without a friend in the world seem to dash through life oblivious to their social condition. Whether due to a naturally introverted personality or a subconscious emotional suppression, they just don't seem to feel lonely. They aren't sitting around waiting to be chosen.

In contrast, you have probably heard of stories where the guy who leads the varsity team, makes straight A's, and dates the head cheerleader suddenly takes his own life. Was he not adored (and even envied) by everyone at school and in town? Did he not belong?

Yes he did, but he didn't believe it, and so he didn't feel it. Even though he was chosen by the team, his teachers, and the most popular girl at school, it wasn't enough. He still felt alone.

The sad truth is many, many married people feel desperately alone.

At one point, two lonely people choose one another. They say those precious words of surrender: I do. Then from that day forward, they brush their teeth every morning, share household chores every day, and go to bed every night with the person who chose them. They even make love sometimes. They never have to worry about finding a date for a party or a wedding. And they share social media posts with their smiling faces eclipsed only by the smiling faces of their adorable children.

But still they feel … alone.

If you don't want this to be you, please don't date to belong.

Jesus Chose You!

If you want to date in a healthy, whole way, you need to know something.

No. You need to *believe* something.

You who long to belong: You already do. You who desire to be chosen: You already have been.

Jesus himself said:

> *You did not choose Me but I chose you, and appointed you that you would go and bear fruit, and that your fruit would remain, so that whatever you ask of the Father in My name He may give to you.*
> —John 15:16 NASB

Until you can believe these words of Jesus, until you truly believe you have been chosen by, and therefore belong to, a God who would give His life for you (and did), you likely won't ever feel like you belong anywhere else.

Why? Because there's no one else in this universe to whom you could ever expect to belong to more than the one who made you for Himself and gave Himself for you.

So, dating to belong is not just a bad idea. It's a hopeless idea.

DUMB REASON #3: ROMANCE

Romance: It's the veritable holy grail of dating.

What could be wrong with romance? An entire book of the Bible is dedicated to celebrating the wonder of romantic/sexual love. And if that doesn't impress you at first, consider this: There is no other book of the Bible dedicated to celebrating any other single topic. There is no book focused on health, education, diet, exercise, finances, race relations, parenting, government, work, economics, war, or creation care.

The only book of the entire Bible dedicated to any one topic is Song of Solomon, and the only topic deemed worthy of the focus of an entire book is, of all things, romantic/sexual love.

That said, the book which celebrates romance and sex issues a warning about pursuing either before you're ready. Indeed, it offers this warning not once, not twice, but three times:

> *Do not stir up or awaken love until the appropriate time.*
> —Song of Solomon 2:7, 3:5, 8:4 CSB

When the promoters of a cause have words of warning regarding that cause, we ought to sit up and take notice, don't you think?

Perhaps, along with their goodness, there is something dangerous about romantic and sexual intimacy, something that demands we handle them with care, something we ought to be ready and maybe even prepare for, intentionally and carefully.

What Romantics Want More than Romance

Romance can be wonderful, like chocolate for the soul. I hope you enjoy a lot of it in your lifetime. When the time is right.

It's delightful to discover someone you like who likes you back, and blissful to share an evening with that person. However, your soul cannot live off of romance alone, any more than your body can live off chocolate alone.

So instead of romance, make relational intimacy the goal of your dating life, because determining whether or not you can establish and grow a meaningful friendship with the person you're dating should be the point of going out with them in the first place.

While relationships which begin as romances can dissolve as quickly as they commenced, a romance that grows out of a genuine friendship is far more likely to last because it's built on mutual trust, respect, and compatibility.

Do You Even Know How to Be Relationally Intimate?

Put simply, intimacy is deeply knowing and being known by someone.

So, while middle school lovers only want to know, "Do you like me?" (because if they do, you can enjoy a romance), the real question mature daters want to know is, "Who are you?" (because if you're well-matched you can enjoy a *relationship*).

However, the reality is most daters out there, even mature adults, don't even know how to be intimate in a healthy way. And pursuing romance will never teach you how. On the contrary, pursuing romance in your dating life will teach you to hide undesirable qualities and perform to keep your love interest.

If at this point, you realize you truly don't know how to be intimate in a healthy and whole way, you have the opportunity to save yourself a lot of needless heartbreak. Seek to grow in relationships with good family, friends, and mentors first, before you test your skills in the wild and risky world of dating.

DUMB REASON #2: SEX

Would you like to know God's will for your dating life?

I mean, for real? And not only for your dating life, but do you simply want to know His will?

Fortunately, our God wants us to know His will even more than we want to know it. In fact, three verses in the Bible explicitly declare, "This is the will of God." And though dating wasn't even a thing in Bible times, one of those verses proffers a very clear direction for your dating life. (I guess you could say God is pretty forward-thinking.)

> *For this is the will of God, your sanctification ...* —1 Thessalonians 4:3a ESV

There it is in black and white. God's will is our sanctification. That means our purity, purification, or holiness.

So, the next natural question is, "How do you date in a pure and holy way?"

Well, we don't have to wonder for long, for Paul clarifies it in the following verses, beginning with the second half of the verse we just read.

> *For this is the will of God, your sanctification:* ***that you abstain from sexual immorality*** *...* —1 Thessalonians 4:3 ESV (emphasis mine)

Paul says if we truly want to follow God's will, we will abstain from sexual immorality. The Greek word for "sexual immorality" is "porneia." It's the root word of "pornography," and refers to any sexual activity outside of marriage. Can you see what this has to do with dating?

Sexual Purity Is Bigger Than Abstinence

Put simply, if you want to follow the will of God in your dating life, you will save sex for marriage. But Paul doesn't just leave us with a "no-no," he wants us to catch a vision for how we should live our lives, and therefore how we should date.

> *For this is the will of God, your sanctification: that you abstain from sexual immorality;* ***that each one of you know how to control his own body in holiness and honor*** *...* —1 Thessalonians 4:3-4 ESV (emphasis mine)

Wow. That's a grander picture of God's will, isn't it? He's not just asking us to refrain from certain naughty things, He's calling us up to become a certain kind of person. Not just a *non*-naughty person, but a person of true integrity, someone who knows *"how to control his own body in holiness and honor."* Is that a tall order? Yes. Indeed, if you do not have God's Holy Spirit inside you, I believe it's an impossible order. However, I also find it inspiring.

The Biblical Sexual Standard Has Always Seemed "Unrealistic"

Regardless of anyone's opinion, let me put one myth to death right here and now—the myth that the moral standards of scripture are no longer applicable because past cultures were somehow less "progressive" than we are today.

On the contrary, according to this passage, the culture in Paul's day wasn't any more chaste than ours is now.

> *For this is the will of God, your sanctification: that you abstain from sexual immorality; that each one of you know how to control his own body in holiness and honor,* **not in the passion of lust like the Gentiles who do not know God** … —1 Thessalonians 4:3-5 ESV (emphasis mine)

I guess you could say that those "who do not know God" have always lived their lives "in the passion of lust." And in Jesus' day, they managed to live so without the prevalence of internet porn.

So if Paul's words applied back then, they apply to us today. Put simply, those who know God should act very differently from those who do not, whenever in history or wherever in the world they find themselves.

Do you really want to know God's will? Well, this is obviously a pretty big deal to Him. And if you're still not convinced, let's continue reading after verse 5:

… that no one transgress and wrong his brother in this matter, because the Lord is an avenger in all these things, as we told you beforehand and solemnly warned you. For God has not called us for impurity, but in holiness. Therefore whoever disregards this, disregards not man but God, who gives his Holy Spirit to you.
—1 Thessalonians 4:6-8 ESV

Sex Is NOT Bad

The understandable (but completely wrong) conclusion many come to from passages like the one above is that sex is bad. But let's remember who came up with the whole idea! Our Creator!

Take note, the passage above from 1 Thessalonians 4 (along with all the many passages like it) is not condemning *sex*. These passages condemn sexual *sin*.

So, it's not sex that is bad, but sexual *sin* that is bad.

Consider fire. Is fire good or bad?

- Fire in the fireplace of your home? Good!
- Fire in the bedroom of your home? Bad!

Is atomic energy good or bad?

- Atomic energy supplying power to your house? Good!
- Atomic energy dropped on top of your house? Bad!

So the reality is this: Sex is far more than good! It is wonderful, powerful, and dangerous.

And it is this "dangerous" element that makes sexual sin so destructive.

DUMB REASON #1: TO *FIND* LOVE

Are you dating, or wanting to date, so you can find love? Do you believe the right romantic relationship will complete something in you that's missing right now?

I believed that myself in the past. But, trust me! After being joyfully married to an amazing woman for over 28 years, I now know that belief is false.

My dear wife, no matter how amazing she is, simply can't understand me and love me as deeply as my soul longs to be known and loved. And she would say the same about me.

This is why we need a love like the love of Jesus.

If I claim to follow Christ but I am dating to *find* love, it reveals I am overestimating the kind of love I can find in another human soul.

Furthermore, I'm overestimating the kind of love I have to offer others, because we're all flawed. Not slightly bent by a few weaknesses, but completely broken by sin. If it were not so, why would Jesus have had to die for us? Why did our redemption require such an awe-inspiring sacrifice? Why not just a little torture? Or better yet, a lot of money?

Because sin brings death—not pain or disappointment or room for improvement—death. That said, left in our sin we have no love to give. Dead people cannot love.

But sink your heart into this amazing truth: The fact that Jesus *was* willing to die for you means you are already loved more profoundly than you ever will be on any date with anyone.

Don't Feel God's Love?

Do you struggle with feeling God's love?

Then do you believe in His love at all? I mean, do you really believe God's love is as great as the Bible declares it is but not great enough to love you?

Just like belonging, love is something you only feel when you believe it. Indeed, when it comes to love, the power of belief is so fierce you can *feel* loved—deeply and completely loved—by someone you've only known for a month. Or a week. Perhaps you've experienced this rush of emotions.

However, while feelings are always real, they're not always right.

Only the One Who Knows You Best Can Love You Most

You can't really love someone you don't know. You can experience loving feelings for them or you can extend loving actions toward them (or both), but the depth of your love is limited by your knowledge of your beloved.

Two young love birds typically hold a very idealized perception of each other. Their feelings may be electric, but they love more of an ideal than the actual identity of their beloved.

In contrast, two old love birds who have celebrated their 50th wedding anniversary know one another like no one else. Their feelings are more firm than fantastic, but they've seen the best and the worst of each other—sometimes brought out both the best and the worst in each other—and have learned to hold onto each other as they honor their vows. Whatever they lack in passion they more than make up for in devotion.

The depth of love is limited by knowledge. This means only the one who knows you best can love you most.

But you don't have to wait for 50 years of marriage to know that kind of love.

Our God is the lover of your soul who knows everything there is to know about you (the good, the bad, and the truly shameful), and He loves you still, enough to die for you.

Hear Jesus' words to His disciples (including you):

> *As the Father has loved me, so have I loved you. Abide in my love.*
> *If you keep my commandments, you will abide in my love, just as*
> *I have kept my Father's commandments and abide in his love.*
> —John 15:9-10 ESV

Do you struggle with believing in God's love for you? Then I would urge you to put your dating life on hold and seek to understand the height and depth, the length and breadth, the richness and intensity, the joy and security, and the wonder and realness of God's love for you.

Then you can date, not to *find* love, but to *share* love with another passionate lover of Jesus. A sinner-saved-by-grace who can love you not just because they find you attractive, funny, or intriguing, but because God's love can't help but flow out of them.

But first you must believe this: You will never find love because Love has already found you! So stop looking for Love and surrender to Him.

This chapter marks the end of the second lesson in an 8-week LoveEd study. For discussion questions and resources go to:

FMUniversity.net/DatePrep-wk2

43

CHAPTER 4:
WHY IT'S SO EASY TO FALL FOR THE WRONG PERSON

In this chapter and the two that follow, we will identify nine Mr. or Ms. Wrongs; that is nine personality profiles you should not date. However, my guess is that for most of them, you might think, "Duh! Why would I want to date somebody like that? Of course I'll avoid them! I'm not desperate."

And yet, seemingly normal, healthy, intelligent individuals wind up dating partners like this every day. Perhaps one of those seemingly normal, healthy, intelligent individuals has even been you … I mean someone you know. Indeed, many wind up even marrying the kind of people I'm about to describe.

What explains this?

It's simple: the kind of traits I'm going to warn you about are not obvious to spot right away, which means that to discern some of these red flags, it will take getting to know your date over a significant period of time.

In the meantime, there will be other *positive* traits about the person you're interested in that you can't ignore:

- They're gorgeous.
- They're easy to talk with.
- They're funny.
- They're into the same things you are.
- They're also into you. A lot.
- They're a great kisser.
- They're kind to woodland creatures.

This is why one of the biggest challenges of dating is looking past the obvious positive qualities your date possesses (or at least presents) to discern the potential presence of negative qualities that are not so obvious. Especially if your date is actively trying to hide these negative traits from you.

If that task wasn't hard enough already, it can be even more difficult if your date's positive qualities have you falling in love with them before you've had a chance to perceive any red flags.

MR. AND MS. WRONG ARE WORTHY OF LOVE TOO!

While everyone is worthy of love, not everyone is ready to handle a serious dating relationship. Looking at it another way, not everyone is mature and healthy enough to handle your heart the way your Heavenly Father would desire.

So, as you read through this list of personality profiles and you recognize someone you know, pray for their good! Pray for them to surrender to Jesus. Pray for them to overcome their challenges, so they can become the person our God made them to be. Not so they can be *yours* someday, but so they can be *His forever*!

And then steer clear of them! Especially if you find yourself attracted to them or you suspect they may be attracted to you.

No, this is not mean. This is wisdom. It's also loving because love wants the best for others.

And here's what's best for every Mr. or Ms. Wrong: mature same-gender friends and mentors in their lives to help them grow and change, without any weird or distracting romantic vibes getting in the way.

I know. In rom-coms, the valiant knight saves the damsel in distress, or the sweet beauty tames the heart of the beast. But your life is not a movie. It is reality. Date in reality. In the end, it's always better that way.

With that background, let's get to our list of nine Mr. or Ms. Wrongs.

MR./MS. WRONG #1: THE STRANGER

When you were a kid, what was the one rule about strangers?

Don't talk to strangers.

Pretty much covers everything, doesn't it? Should you get in a car with a stranger? Accept candy from a stranger? Hold their hand?

No. NO. NO! You're not even supposed to talk with them. But then you get into the dating world and suddenly strangers are no longer a danger. Heck, they might be the love of your life!

As a result, you are not only encouraged to talk with them, it's considered completely normal to get in a car with a stranger and travel to an undisclosed location for an indeterminate amount of time, where you will eat and drink with them, engage in personal conversation with them, and maybe even make out with them. Or more!

Of course, one of the reasons you date is to get to know someone better, but there's a huge difference between dating to get to know a friend better, or even to get to know an acquaintance better, and dating to get to know a stranger for the first time.

So here is **Dating Commandment #1: Thou shalt not date strangers.** And to be clear, a stranger is anyone who neither you nor anyone you know and trust knows and trusts.

If you don't really know someone, you shouldn't trust them either unless one or more of your friends knows and trusts them. Otherwise, the person in question is a stranger and not a qualified dating candidate.

Sound too legalistic? Then you should know about an online survey we conducted where we asked college students and young adults to share their first-date horror stories. Boy did we get some whoppers!

However, when I considered all the crazy tales, it occurred to me that there was one rule—just one rule—that if followed, could have prevented every single first date fail. Every one!

And thus our first Dating Commandment was born.

How to Get to Know Someone Before the First Date

Am I saying you should run away from anyone you don't know like you were taught when you were five? No!

Should you ignore them? Shun them? Consider them dead to you?

No. No. And no.

So, what's a body to do if they want to date someone they don't know from Adam?

Get to know them *first*, before the first date. Ingenious, right?

Hang out with them in the company of people you *do* know and trust, so you can all get to know this "person of interest" together. That way, they can also get to know you and your friends. It's even better if their friends come along for the fun.

If you meet online, it's a lot trickier. Especially if you've met on a dating site, where romantic hopes are already a thing from the first contact. But we strongly suggest opening up your entire text/chat/DM/email history to a couple of friends or mentors. Don't hide anything from those who know you best and love you most!

Online predation is real! As is the common practice of catfishing.

And speaking of catfishing, it isn't necessarily intentional deception. We are all naturally inclined to project who we wish we were, so it's often more self-deception than fraud.

I don't say that to minimize online pretense, but more to point out that almost all of us are guilty of projecting an online image that doesn't quite match reality or only matches it in our best moments. Think how much more pretense there could be with someone who is intentionally hoping to lure an unsuspecting victim into falling for them.

The Three Things You Want to Know Before Your First Date

If you're determined to not date strangers, you (or someone you know and trust) should be fairly familiar with the following before the first date:

1. Your potential date's character
2. Your potential date's friends
3. What your potential date's friends think about their character

Will this information take some amount of time to gather, especially in a comfortable, casual way that doesn't feel like an interview process?

Yes, but think of what you stand to gain: no more first date fails. And though it won't ensure a pain-free dating life, sticking to this one dating commandment will result in far less heartbreak, rejection, and regret.

Consider what happened to Joseph and the Israelites when they were duped into making a treaty with the Gibeonites (as recorded in Joshua 9).

WHY IT'S SO EASY TO FALL FOR THE WRONG PERSON

They made what seemed at the time a completely logical decision based on how the Gibeonites looked and the story they told. It reminds me a lot of how people get hoodwinked in dating all the time.

MR./MS. WRONG #2: THE VIOLENT PERSON

A person with a violent temper needs therapy. Not another victim.

And that is precisely what you become when you date the violent person. Just ask the last person they dated.

Violent people don't get better through dating. And I have this on good authority, as I've spoken with a plethora of counselors, pastors, and therapists, and not a single one has reported a session that went like this:

Patient: *I really struggle with rage.*

Counselor: *Are you currently dating anyone?*

Patient: *No. My temper largely ended my last relationship. I loved them, but I think they were more or less terrified of me. That's sort of why I'm here.*

Counselor: *Well, obviously, they weren't the right one for you then. We need to get you dating again straight away! Let's get on Tinder together right now!*

There is no such thing as dating therapy. There *is* such a thing as enabling someone to continue in destructive behavior.

Enduring Abuse Is NOT the Same Thing as Sacrifice

True love demands sacrifice, yielding to what's best for your beloved, a giving of yourself, sometimes even laying down your life for your beloved. And that usually hurts. However, for love to be love—even when it must hurt—it must be freely given. Jesus, who made the ultimate sacrifice, is our example.

For this reason the Father loves me, because I lay down my life that I may take it up again. No one takes it from me, but I lay it down of my own accord. I have authority to lay it down, and I have authority to take it up again. This charge I have received from my Father. —John 10:17-18 ESV

Sacrifice is about the other's best interests, believing that what is truly best for the other is best for you and for everyone, while abuse is about no one's best interest. In the end, no one is better off, not even the abuser for getting whatever it was they wanted.

- **Sacrifice** is redemptive,
  while **abuse** is destructive.

- **Sacrifice** is chosen,
  while **abuse** is forced.

- **Sacrifice** is anticipated in faith,
  while **abuse** is dreaded with fear.

- **Sacrifice** is endured with courage,
  while **abuse** is endured in desperation.

- **Sacrifice** leads to joy for all,
  while **abuse** leads to misery for all.

This is why marriage is such a good and glorious idea: an opportunity for two people to commit to seeking the other's best interests at every turn in a relationship of redemption. Where a man and a woman choose to love, honor, and cherish each other for life, anticipating in faith not only the better, the richer, and the health but also the worse, the poorer, and the sickness, so they can endure every sacrifice with courage, and walk in joy as they keep their marriage vows together.

What Constitutes Abuse?

On the flip side, the idea of abuse in our modern culture has been watered down so significantly that almost anyone can claim to be a victim. And many do.

Indeed, in a culture where simply disagreeing with someone can be considered hate speech, victims are legion.

That said, can we at least agree on this? No one should fear for their physical safety when dating. To put it in concrete terms, any date where you are ever physically harmed or even threatened by your partner should be the last date with that individual. Are you with me?

Dating Commandment #2: Thou shalt not tolerate even one threat of physical violence.

If This Is Their "Best Behavior," Who Wants to See Their Worst?

An important point to remember when it comes to tolerating abuse: most are on their best behavior when dating or in the throes of romantic affection. Usually, the darker side of a person comes out later. Often much later. So if you're already being hurt or threatened while you're dating, where do you think that's going to lead later in your relationship?

I realize many truly wonderful people have a problem with their temper. If you've fallen in love with someone like that, you can be tempted to give them a pass. And then another. And then another. But don't!

Remember, dating therapy is not a thing. Stay. Away. From. The. Violent. Person.

And if you know anyone who has been physically harmed or threatened on a date, warn them and help them get away and get help.

MR./MS. WRONG #3: THE SEXUALLY PROMISCUOUS PERSON

The sexually promiscuous person needs prayer. Not prey. And that's just what you are to the sexually promiscuous person. Just ask the last person they dated.

Again, like the violent person, the sexually experienced person (who's looking to add to their résumé) can be wonderful in almost every other way. They might even love Jesus almost as much as they love sex.

But please stay away from them.

You may believe you are going to hold the standard, but you must understand that the value you place on your sexual purity (and your passion to defend it) is one of the things that will make you such an attractive mark to the sexually promiscuous person.

Indeed, I was sharing this list of Mr. and Ms. Wrongs with a group of college counselors when one of them disclosed, "I have a client I'm working with who confessed he likes to date really sweet Christian girls and work them down."

In this sense, the rest of the animal kingdom is much smarter than we large-brained humans are. They know to avoid predators.

How Much Messing Around Is OK?

It can almost seem noble for a sincere Christian person who prizes sexual purity to date someone who doesn't prize it—in the hopes of showing them a different way. Almost like witnessing to them.

But there's something very broken about this thinking. Dating a person who doesn't share your sexual standards already requires lowering your standards to date them!

> *But among you there must not be even a hint of sexual immorality,*
> *or of any kind of impurity, or of greed, because these are improper*
> *for God's holy people.* —Ephesians 5:3 NIV

Not even a *hint* of sexual immorality. That's a tall order!

Wouldn't you agree that a dating relationship where one partner openly rejects the beauty and significance of sexual holiness gives off more than a hint of sexual immorality?

Dating Commandment #3 is hence: Thou shalt not tolerate even a hint of sexual immorality.

Standards Were Never Meant to Be Held Alone

Sexual purity is hard enough to maintain between two believers committed to making it happen. With God as our witness, my wife and I desperately wanted to be sexually pure when we were dating, but we clearly weren't committed enough. We remained virgins until our wedding night, but we gave in to sexual temptation time and time again.

If either of us had been of the mind, "What are we waiting for?" we never would have made it.

Standards are standards for a reason. They're supposed to set your priorities, determine your boundaries, limit your options, and direct your decisions. And any relationship—dating, family, friendship, business—calls for everyone to hold up the standards together.

Are You Fleeing or Freeing Sexual Immorality?

> *Flee from sexual immorality. Every other sin a person commits is*
> *outside the body, but the sexually immoral person sins against his*
> *own body.* —1 Corinthians 6:18 ESV

God's word tells us to "flee" sexual immorality, but when we date the sexually promiscuous person, we do the exact opposite of God's command. We *free* temptation. Fleeing sexual immorality requires steering clear of the sexually promiscuous person.

THE GOAL OF DATING IS NOT TO MAKE THE "PERFECT" CHOICE

Before we continue this lineup of the usual suspects, allow me to give you some more perspective. For one thing, your goal in dating should never be to make the perfect choice.

This is true for at least three reasons:

1. The perfect choice is impossible to make.
2. The perfect choice does not exist.
3. The perfect choice cannot be found.

Of course, that was all the same reason but in different words, but my point is for you to embrace this truth. Then, instead of making the *perfect* choice, seek to make a *wise* choice.

You might think, despite its loftiness, aiming for perfection is the better goal. (It's certainly the higher goal.) You might think if you shoot for perfection, you're more likely to get what you want.

But consider this perspective in other pursuits. For instance, your dream car and the car you need are likely two very different vehicles, and insisting on your dream car will likely lead to one of two outcomes:

1. You, "rideless" for the remainder of your life

2. You, in debt for the remainder of your life, perhaps paying on a note for a vehicle that's as impractical (and as expensive to maintain) as it is beautiful

Hoping for fantasy seldom leads someone to a good place in reality.

THE REAL DANGER OF LOOKING FOR
THE "PERFECT" PERSON

It would be bad enough if looking for the perfect partner kept you forever searching and forever single, but the scary thing is that looking for the perfect partner can often lead you to fall for someone—and even marry someone—who's *far* from perfect. Someone who's unhealthy, even dangerous.

How can this be?

Because the illogical and idealistic criteria behind the search for the perfect mate will lead you to follow your feelings instead of following the facts. People who trust God to give them the perfect mate will "sense God leading them" to make rash and foolish choices. I've seen it time and time again, in both dating and marriage.

So, the whole point of this list of Mr./Ms. Wrongs is to guide you in making a wise choice by removing nine different personality profiles from consideration.

WHY WE DON'T REALLY WANT TO MAKE
WISE DATING DECISIONS

Once, when discussing this list of Mr./Ms. Wrongs in class, a student blurted out, "Well you don't want to ask too many questions when you're dating because you don't want to mess anything up."

The whole class burst into laughter because, of course, how could asking wise questions "mess anything up?"

Or maybe they burst into laughter because everyone could relate. We all understand the temptation to turn a blind eye to red flags so we can enjoy the fun of a relationship as long as it will last. Even if it probably *won't* last. Even if it *shouldn't* last.

Why do we do this? Why do we shun prudence in one of the most important endeavors of our lives: the mission we hope will lead us to the person we expect to spend the rest of our lives with?

The simple (and sad) truth: wisdom seldom brings immediate gratification.

Falling in love can happen just like that. There couldn't be anything more gratifying in the world than discovering someone you're crushing on is crushing on you. Only harder.

But are the good vibes in the moment worth the heartache and regret that must naturally follow poor decisions? Especially poor dating decisions?

Think about it. If you're dating someone who isn't good for you, someone who can't communicate clearly and honestly, or someone who isn't even ready for a serious relationship with anyone, don't you want to "mess up" the relationship sooner rather than later?

Either way, there's a price to be paid. The price for wisdom is usually paid up front, in the form of delayed gratification. The price of folly is usually paid later, in the form of heartache, rejection, and regret.

CHAPTER 5:

YOU SHOULDN'T DATE PEOPLE TO CHANGE THEM

It is common for a typically rational human being to fall in love with someone possessing glaring character defects because they believe they can change that person. They may even believe it is their mission to do so.

But you shouldn't date people to change them.

It is true that many people have discovered the motivation to change in dramatically positive ways, only after falling in love with some angelic being (like yourself, perhaps).

However, those who experience a rapid change in core character qualities can revert to earlier patterns just as rapidly. I'm not saying they *will* revert, but it shouldn't be surprising if they do.

JESUS DIDN'T CHANGE PEOPLE BY DATING THEM

Even Jesus didn't employ dating as a tool for changing anyone. He had to *die* for them. Literally. And even that wasn't enough. Then He had to rise from the dead. Again, literally.

You could conceivably give your life for your date, but you can't conquer death, which means you can't conquer the demons hiding in the history and heart of your date.

In light of this truth, you can see how presumptive it would be to date one of the personality profiles we're going to warn you about, believing you can help them change. Or even believing that you *should* help them change.

You might, but the odds are against it. And even if you do, the change likely won't be permanent. Am I making sense? If so, then dating any of these nine Mr./Ms. Wrongs doesn't make any sense. Here are the next three.

MR./MS. WRONG #4: THE LONER

Know that pretty and precious wallflower? How about that tall, dark, and handsome lone wolf?

Do. Not. Date. Them.

I realize this prohibition can seem cruel, like denying water to a person dying of thirst, but giving romantic love to a lonely person is *not* like giving water to someone who's dehydrated. It's like giving them hard liquor.

The person dying of thirst needs water. Not liquor. And the loner needs a friend. Not a romantic interest.

I know. I know. A good dating partner should be a good friend. But that's not the *kind* of friend a loner needs.

It can seem like you are helping the loner at first because, obviously, a loner isn't lonely when they're in love with someone who loves them back.

However, ultimately there are only two outcomes to dating a loner:

1. Break up: leaving the loner even lonelier than before with no relationship base to encourage them and help them move forward without you

2. Marriage: leaving you obligated for life to meet all the relational needs of the loner since they have no relational support system to support them and your marriage

And believe you me, every marriage needs a relational support system for encouragement, accountability, and guidance.

But when you're in the throes of romantic passion you don't feel that need. Like who can even *think* about friends when you have a significant other to daydream about every waking moment you aren't with them?

So by dating the loner, you keep them feeling good about themselves, even as you keep them from growing in the kind of relationships they need most. This is why **Dating Commandment #4 is as follows: Thou shalt not put romance ahead of friendship.**

Why Loners Make Passionate Lovers. But Bad Ones.

Why would you be tempted to date a loner?

A. They're gorgeous
B. They want to date you
C. You have a heart that bleeds for lonely people

Then there's a reality that makes loners particularly passionate lovers, namely that their neediness can make them fiercely devoted to you, which can feel great. Indeed, it can make you feel incredibly special.

You could wind up with loads of gifts, encouraging texts throughout the day, and little notes hidden in your home and car.

However, a devotion born out of neediness isn't really about you. It's about them. So, in essence, they're using you. All the attention they shower on you is less about how they feel about you and more about how you make them feel about *themselves*.

But eventually, one of two things will happen:

1. The newness of the romance will wear off, and the reality that one person can never fill all the relational needs of another will become apparent to the loner.

2. The neediness of the loner will wear on you, and the reality that one person can never fill all the relational needs of another will become apparent to *you*.

How to Spot a Loner

Be aware, not all loners are obvious.

Some clearly have no friends. They may know it and even be open about it. These are usually your introverted loners.

However, other loners, the extroverted types, can seem to have a lot of friends. They may even be the "life of the party," but you eventually discover they keep people at arm's length and aren't close to anyone.

But they'd like to get close to you.

Because you're nice to look at. And fun to kiss.

So, what does it take to spot a loner? Time. Careful discernment over time.

It might feel all wrong to throw the brakes on an epic love story, but according to the love chapter of the Bible, 1 Corinthians 13, love is first and foremost patient! So, if you're feeling rushed, you aren't being led by love.

MR./MS. WRONG #5: THE FOOL

There's nothing wrong with possessing a low IQ. There's also nothing wrong with being simple or naïve. But there is something wrong with being a fool.

By "fool," I'm talking about someone who lacks sense, wisdom, discretion, and self-control. Someone who can't seem to connect cause and effect. Or they can see the connection, but they just can't seem to keep from hurting themselves. As Proverbs 26 so eloquently states:

> *Like a dog that returns to its vomit, So is a fool who repeats his foolishness.* —Proverbs 26:11 NASB

They might be openly rebellious, flouting any authority or reason, or they might fly under the radar as an underachiever who's content to just get by.

However they present it outwardly, inwardly the fool is motivated by impulse—a slave to their passions and lusts. Because of this, they are likely enslaved to addictive behaviors like drugs, alcohol, debt, gambling, or porn.

This being the case, the fool needs help—not someone's heart. Indeed, giving your heart to a fool is like giving flowers to a cow. They'll enjoy it … as they consume it.

What You're in for When You Date a Fool

Proverbs has a lot to say about the "perks" (read: baggage) that come with dating a fool. Amongst other defining characteristics are the following:

- Always right in their own eyes (Proverbs 12:15)

- Can't help but demonstrate foolishness (Proverbs 13:16)

- Arrogant and careless (Proverbs 14:16)

- Undisciplined (Proverbs 15:5)

- Would rather voice their opinion than seek understanding (Proverbs 18:2)

- Loves to fight (Proverbs 20:3)

- Gives full vent to their temper (Proverbs 29:11)

As Proverbs 17 puts it:

> *He who fathers a fool does so to his sorrow, And the father of a fool has no joy.* —Proverbs 17:21 NASB

How can the father of a fool have no joy while someone else can fall in love and date that same fool and enjoy it?

Perhaps the answer lies in the amount of time spent with the fool. A father has likely known the fool since day one. It's probably not a bad idea to consider how those who have known your love interest their entire life feel about them.

Can You Help a Fool by Dating Them?

The fool needs to understand two things:

1. They have a problem—likely several

2. Solving their problem(s) will require significant change on their part

But do you want to know what will keep the fool from this essential realization?

Distractions.

This is the explanation behind all the fool's self-medicating behaviors: drugs, alcohol, etc. This is how even something as benign as video games can become an obsession. And what more obsessive distraction could a fool find than a romantic partner?!

This means when you date a fool, you hurt them instead of helping them— by becoming a new distraction. A far more attractive distraction.

A kissy-kissy relationship with you gives the fool a chemical high of infatuation that's better than drugs, a winning feeling that beats any payout, and a physical and emotional connection far more real than the fantasy of porn.

This is why many fools can quit their addictions cold-turkey when they fall in love.

For a season.

But the root problems, of which the self-medicating behaviors were only symptoms, remain. So when the infatuation fades, the thrill of winning your heart is old hat, and the excitement of seeing your face becomes commonplace, the old habits beckon.

And as this happens, you become either disgusted with them or desperate for them, driving them back to their distractions of choice.

Maybe into the arms of a new love.

You "Love" Them, but Do You Respect Them?

A guy might say about his girl, "She's a goddess! It's like Jennifer Aniston and Scarlett Johansson had a baby! I mean, if that were possible. Plus she says the funniest things. We laugh all the time. **Of course, sometimes I'm laughing *at* her because she's kind of an airhead."**

Or a girl might say about her guy, "He plays drums in a band, and they just got signed to a record label! And the best part? He treats me like a queen! **Of course, it's a good thing he's so talented because he's not the sharpest tool in the shed."**

Again, there is nothing wrong with dating someone simple or naïve, but there is something wrong with dating someone you don't respect.

If you're dating someone because you like how they look, how they make you laugh, how talented they are, or how they make you feel, but you don't respect them, then you're using them.

And using people is generally frowned on in most cultures. As it should be!

Mutual Chemistry Proves Nothing

When you think about it, the proof of a great relationship is mutual respect. This is true in *any* relationship: family, friend, work, or romance. If the relationship is healthy, mutual respect will be one of the fruits.

Mutual respect is something solid and dependable. It grows out of the character of those in the relationship, character revealed by the choices made by the individuals in the relationship which are guided by sincerely held values, convictions, priorities, and goals.

In contrast, our culture says the evidence of a great romantic relationship is not mutual respect but mutual chemistry.

No doubt, mutual chemistry is fun to experience, whether it's between two lovers sharing coffee or two performers sharing a stage, but unlike the solidity of mutual respect, mutual chemistry is hard to measure and hard to explain. Those who share mutual chemistry just seem to know it. They simply enjoy one another's company; they click. They might even be able to finish each other's sentences or sandwiches. I don't know, but it's good.

However, the problem with looking to mutual chemistry as the proof of a great relationship is that chemistry tends to be as unreliable as it is unexplainable.

So, here's **Dating Commandment #5: Thou shalt not prize mutual chemistry above mutual respect.**

It's not just a romance thing. You probably know besties who became frenemies overnight. Or friends who thought they'd make the greatest roommates until they *were* roommates. And now they're no longer friends.

So don't date a fool for the simple reason that you cannot respect a fool.

MR./MS. WRONG #6: THE DECEIVER

You would think warning people not to date a deceiver would be like warning people not to date an alligator. No one wants to get too close to an alligator. Who would want to do so with someone they couldn't trust?

However, in many romantic dramas and rom-coms, Hollywood presents deceit as the source of both humor and tension. It might be a simple misunderstanding that the partner who knows the truth can't bring themselves to clear up for fear of losing their lover. Or it could be a series of white lies one person tells the other out of desperation to "win their heart." Or the best stories (read: most ridiculous) are those where someone initially sets out to defraud someone else (or even kill them) but then falls in love with them in the process.

Now that's the setup for a fabulous relationship, right? No!

Regardless, this narrative sends the message that it might not only be necessary to deceive someone to keep them in a relationship, it could be noble. And in the end, when the truth finally comes out, everything's good because it was all done "in the name of love."

But while deception may be funny to watch, it's less funny to experience.

Again, truth isn't just a casual preference of most healthy people, it is the lifeblood of healthy relationships. In fact, I've known many people who justified divorce because of broken trust, proclaiming, "If there's no trust, there's no relationship."

The reality is you *can* have a relationship without any trust, just not a good one. So, take a cue from my divorced friends, and don't tolerate in dating what you would refuse to tolerate in marriage. Even if it looks funny in the movies.

That might be why one of the ten commandments prohibits bearing false witness. And it's certainly why **Dating Commandment #6 is thus: Thou shalt not bear nor tolerate false witness.**

> *Do not lie to one another, seeing that you have put off the old self with its practices and have put on the new self, which is being renewed in knowledge after the image of its creator.* —Colossians 3:9-10 ESV

Beware of First Impressions

The way we go about romantic relationships makes it easy for a deceiver to get away with murder. Or at least romanticide.

The problem begins with basic human nature because our unconscious tendency whenever we first meet someone is to use what little we learn about them to fill in the blanks of what we don't know.

Add "attraction" to the mix, and your mind can be made up before you know it, filling in a ton of blanks in an overly positive way. (They call it "love at first sight.")

However, the real problem comes from basing the level of trust we place in someone on the personality profile we've created in our minds, instead of basing our level of trust on the actual information we possess.

For instance, after meeting someone at a party, you might know the following (**concrete facts in bold**):

- They are attractive.
- **Where they went to school**
- **Where they work**
- They are *really* attractive.
- **Where they grew up**
- **How many siblings they grew up with**
- Their eyes are like pools of love and their smile lights up your life.
- **They speak English.** And their voice is like that of an angel.
- **They know karate.** And may be a superhero in disguise.
- You would like to see them in their superhero karate outfit.

Q: How much trust should you be willing to place in a person you know this well?

A: As much as you would any other acquaintance of whom you know fairly little.

However, the summary profile you might construct from your 30 minutes of conversation with this new person reads like this: They are one of the kindest, funniest, smartest, most interesting, most capable people you have ever met in your life. And they *might* even be the one you're supposed to marry.

Q: How much trust are you willing to place in a person you describe like this?

A: Enough to give them your heart. And maybe your body.

Yet any of the following information could also be true about the same person:

- They are obsessed with their appearance.

- They barely graduated from school.

- They have never been happy anywhere they've worked.

- Their parents divorced after an affair, and they have never forgiven them.

- One of their siblings is an alcoholic.

- They smile a lot because they believe you have to "fake it to make it."

- They like to talk a lot and do not listen very well.

- Their interest in karate was inspired by a childhood bully whom they always wanted to wax off.

- They are more likely to be a supervillain than a superhero.

If you had learned all of the above in your first meeting, you might have walked away with an entirely different first impression. But you didn't, so you didn't.

Yet you're already considering what you would name your children.

How to Keep from Being Fooled In Love

If you don't want to be fooled by a deceiver, then you need to take your time, and proceed with a certain level of caution in every dating relationship, being attuned to these qualities in the person you're interested in:

- Reliability—Do they consistently meet reasonable expectations?

- Honesty—Do they tell the truth, completely, even when it's uncomfortable or disadvantages them?

- Clarity—Are misunderstandings so common that you can't be certain if they keep lying to you or you keep misinterpreting them?

- Commitment—Are they committed to the right people and the right things, even when those commitments cost them more than they anticipated?

- Integrity—Are they the same person in different situations and different relationships, or do they seem more "chameleon-like," adjusting their behavior to their current environment?

A clear violation of any of the above should suffice as a blazing red flag.

Bottom line, how much you trust someone should be directly tied to how well you actually know them. So keep your eyes and ears wide open on every date. You know, like you were driving a car and could get hurt if you weren't paying attention.

CHAPTER 6:
YOU MIGHT ALREADY KNOW "THE ONE"

Before we finish our lineup of nine Mr./Ms. Wrongs, we need to remember the wrong person isn't the only one who's difficult to recognize.

The *right* person can be just as hard to spot! In fact, I see healthy, intelligent people make this mistake all the time. They could be staring right at someone who'd be perfect for them!

- Someone who is attractive
- Someone who loves God more than chocolate
- Someone who has thriving relationships with family and friends
- Someone who thinks of other's interests ahead of their own
- Someone who is fun to be around and yet growing in maturity

A dating prospect could be all that and more, yet the person who should be dating them doesn't recognize their marriage potential. They just see the person as a friend.

And I've no room to judge! I once gave my wife the "friends talk."

But don't you judge either! Because I could be talking about YOU!

ARE YOUR EXPECTATIONS REALISTIC?

You might already know someone with whom you could build a fantastic relationship that could lead to a life-giving, lifelong marriage, but they simply don't look like the person you thought you would marry:

- They aren't a supermodel.

- They lack the obvious charm of the protagonist from a Hallmark movie.

- They don't have a big enough social media following.

- They make less money than you do.

- They are allergic to peanuts. And cats. And home improvement shows.

- They fall outside your ideal parameters for height and weight.

Even worse, sometimes Mr. or Ms. Right may have all the above—and check even more important boxes—but if the relationship doesn't begin with the perfect "meet cute" Hollywood has conditioned us to demand, they aren't the one we're looking for.

With that perspective, I encourage you to mind your expectations and keep your heart wide open to who God might have you marry. Until you discover the person you're interested in (or already) dating is one of these nine Mr. or Ms. Wrongs. Then part ways clearly, but kindly. Speaking of, let's finish our list!

MR./MS. WRONG #7: THE INSECURE PERSON

Everyone harbors insecurities, but the insecure person is *defined* by their insecurities.

The insecure person needs prayer, good friends, and mentors, and maybe even counseling. But what they do *not* need is a life preserver. And that is what you become when you date the insecure person. You become their source of confidence and significance and maybe even their source of identity.

Dating Commandment #7: Thou shalt not derive your identity from your dating life. Or your date.

Why We Like to Be Needed

Oh to have someone who belongs to you! Who doesn't like belongings? Especially a "belonging" which is a living human being that adores you whenever you're around and thinks about you whenever you *aren't* around. It's almost like having a pet who can engage in intelligent speech.

But the insecure person doesn't just belong to you, they *need* you! And who doesn't want to be needed?

This makes the early stages of a dating relationship with an insecure person a win-win for everybody. You give them a sense of confidence, significance, and maybe even identity. In return …

- They boost *your* confidence. (*They need me.*)
- They give *you* significance. (*They really need me!*)
- They even give *you* a special superhero-like identity. (*I'm the one who makes their life worth living. They even told me so.*)

However, when you date the insecure person, you wind up using them.

You should delight in the person you're dating simply for who they are. Not for who they think *you* are. When you delight in the importance your date ascribes to you and their relationship with you, you're actually delighting in yourself. (*I'm the kind of person my significant other couldn't do without! I must be pretty neat!*)

A Dating Relationship ≠ A Discipleship Relationship

When you date the insecure person, you can inadvertently distract them from seeking their confidence, significance, and identity in God alone. Yes, even if you're intentionally trying to disciple your significant other.

Why? Because your romantic relationship becomes the evidence of God's love *for* them and their significance *to* Him. If not the only evidence, certainly the most convincing.

So the strength of your significant other's relationship with God becomes tied to the strength of your dating relationship. When things are good between you two, they love God and feel His love. When things are not so good, doubt, fear, and maybe even anger and bitterness toward God arise.

Then if your relationship ends, and it almost always will (more on that in a minute), then the evidence of God's love for them goes down with your relationship.

How Can You Tell If Someone Is Insecure?

Dater beware: the insecure person may not appear insecure on the surface. Instead, they may seem uber-confident. Maybe overconfident.

I was highly insecure until my late teens. (Of course, this is true of most teenagers, which is one of the reasons why most teenagers shouldn't date.)

However, I don't believe I came across that way to most because I used humor to cover my insecurities. I even directed much of my humor at myself. This can give off the appearance of confidence because confident people can laugh at themselves and even enjoy others laughing at them.

However, in practice, I was drawing my sense of value from my ability to get others to laugh (even if at my own expense), while at the same time discouraging criticism by pointing out my weaknesses before others had the chance to do so.

So how can you tell the truly secure person from the impostor? Again, it's the same simple process that empowers you to discern the honest person from the impersonator: Take. Your. Time.

MR./MS. WRONG #8: THE CONTROLLER

Here are five signs you are dating a controller:

1. They don't only want to dominate the conversation.
   They want to dominate your *mind*.

2. They don't only want to share their opinion.
   They want *you* to share their opinion.

3. They don't only want to influence you.
   They want to *manipulate* you.

4. They don't only want to check in on you.
   They want to *supervise* you.

5. They don't only want your time together to revolve around them.
   They want your *whole life* to revolve around them.

Sounds like a relationship of perpetual delight, right? Or maybe terror.

Learn from Samson. He fell for a manipulative maiden named Delilah. She sapped every ounce of will from him, and in the end, she was more or less the death of him. You can check out the whole sordid tale in Judges 16.

How You Wind Up Dating a Controller

Why wouldn't a healthy person avoid a controller like the plague? Or zombies? Or a barren wasteland? Or a barren wasteland filled with zombies carrying the plague?

First, the positive qualities of the controller (their good looks, charm, and talents) can overshadow their controlling ways early on.

Secondly, their controlling ways might not even be employed at first. Not because they're trying to hide them, but because they don't *need* them at first. When you're falling in love, most just want to enjoy the ride, including the controller.

However, when the love chemistry begins to subside or you note red flags you missed before and the controller senses they might be losing you, their manipulative, desperate ways will be revealed. **This is why Dating Commandment #8 is thus: Thou shalt not treat red flags like they are part of a carnival.**

A third reason you may not feel controlled at first? For a controller to know how to control you well, they first have to *know* you well. They have to get to know your family, friends, work hours, workout routines, church commitments, and hobbies.

In that season when the controller is getting to know you, it doesn't feel like control. It feels like attention. Indeed, you really don't know attention until you've had the attention of a controller. It can make you feel pretty special, at first. But once the whole motive behind all that attention is exposed, it can feel constricting—even suffocating—real fast.

The controller might even move from manipulation to threatening to hurt you or harm themselves if you leave the relationship. If so, get a responsible third party involved immediately! You may want to pacify them, but their goal is to control you, so appeasement requires giving them nothing less than control.

MR./MS. WRONG #9: THE UNBELIEVER

And we finally come to it: the ninth of nine Mr. and Ms. Wrongs: the unbeliever.

Do not be unequally yoked with unbelievers. For what partnership has righteousness with lawlessness? Or what fellowship has light with darkness? —2 Cor 6:14 ESV

5 Popular Reasons for Dating an Unbeliever

Reason #1: Doesn't Jesus call us to love *everyone*?

Yes, He does. Sacrificially, *not* romantically. There's a big difference between the two kinds of love.

> *This is my commandment, that you love one another as I have loved you. Greater love has no one than this, that someone lay down his life for his friends.* —John 15:12-13 ESV

Reason #2: This person is more Christian than most Christians I know.

Sadly, I can totally believe that, but sin doesn't make people bad. It makes them dead. We are not *bad* in our sin without Jesus. We are *dead*.

Dating physically dead people is discouraged in every known culture. God feels just as strongly about dating spiritually dead people.

> *For the wages of sin is death, but the free gift of God is eternal life in Christ Jesus our Lord.* —Romans 6:23 ESV

Reason #3: God led me into this relationship.

God's Spirit will *never* lead you to disobey God's Word. It is true that the Spirit led Jesus into the desert to be tempted by the Devil himself. However, the goal wasn't for Jesus to *yield* to temptation but to *resist* temptation. And, in the power of God's same Spirit, He did!

> *Then Jesus said to him, "Be gone, Satan! For it is written, "You shall worship the Lord your God and him only shall you serve."* —Matthew 4:10 ESV

Reason #4: The Bible only says not to *marry* unbelievers, but I'm only going to *date* them.

So if you're not going to marry them, why are you dating them?

Are you "practice dating," where you date someone you'd never marry, so you can be more prepared and confident when you date Mr. or Ms. Right? Is it right to use someone like that? Is that what Jesus would do?

Why not keep the relationship platonic? Are you being honest with yourself? Are you being honest with them?

> *Submit yourselves therefore to God. Resist the devil, and he will flee from you. Draw near to God, and he will draw near to you. Cleanse your hands, you sinners, and purify your hearts, you double-minded.* —James 4:7-8 ESV

Reason #5: I'm dating to witness to them!

So your real goal is not romance but evangelism. Is this the new door-to-door witnessing?

> *Has the Lord as great delight in burnt offerings and sacrifices, as in obeying the voice of the Lord? Behold, to obey is better than sacrifice, and to listen than the fat of rams.* —1 Samuel 15:22 ESV

Every Unbeliever Needs a Savior

Wise individual, please listen to me. The unbeliever is just like us before we believed.

> *For the mind that is set on the flesh is hostile to God, for it does not submit to God's law; indeed, it cannot. Those who are in the flesh cannot please God. You, however, are not in the flesh but in the Spirit, if in fact the Spirit of God dwells in you. Anyone who does not have the Spirit of Christ does not belong to him.* —Romans 8:7-9 ESV

We once lived in darkness. We once didn't belong to Jesus. We once thought we were fine without Him. But that was before we understood our sin and His holiness. That was before we grasped our great need and His great grace.

Tempted to date an unbeliever? Remember the truth: the unbeliever needs a Savior.

And. You. Aren't. Him.

The Bible's Only Guideline for Who You Should Marry

Here's the dealio. Despite the extensive content of this book, there is actually only one scriptural guideline for marriage partner selection, and this is it:

> *Do not be unequally yoked with unbelievers. For what partnership has righteousness with lawlessness? Or what fellowship has light with darkness?* —2 Corinthians 6:14 ESV

"Do not be unequally yoked with unbelievers." That's a farming metaphor that was clearer in Jesus' day when everyone used oxen to pull their plow or knew someone who did. However, when two animals who are not equally matched in strength are teamed up together, the stronger animal winds up doing most of the work, and in the end, as the weaker beast of burden tires, the team is likely to head off course.

This illustration perfectly describes what takes place in a marriage where one partner is seeking to live for Christ and the other isn't. Either the believer continues to strive valiantly to walk the hard road of faith alone, or they find their spiritual life drifting off course entirely.

When talking to widows, Paul simplified this one marriage guideline down to just four little words:

> *A wife is bound to her husband as long as he lives. But if her husband dies, she is free to be married to whom she wishes, **only in the Lord**.* —1 Corinthians 7:39 ESV (emphasis mine)

"Only in the Lord." That's it. The end.

So though I've warned you to avoid nine different personality profiles, the unbeliever is the only one scripture *commands* us to avoid. If we aren't going to take this one clear, specific instruction seriously, why do we look to God's word for advice on dating at all? Or *anything* at all?

Dating Commandment #9: Thou shalt not be unequally yoked.

Do You Want God to Use Your Life? How?

Some violate this principle and God still uses it. Samson, the Israelite judge, did so.

But God can use *anything*! And He *does* use *everything*. God used Samson's lustful desire for worldly women to "provoke the Philistines." What that involved, however, was Samson's betrayal at the hands of the women he loved, which ultimately led to his abduction, the gouging out of his eyes, and his enslavement. Is that the sort of relational future you were hoping for?

Of course, maybe things turn out better for you than for Samson, but how do you *want* to be used by God? In your obedience or in your rebellion?

Either way, God is going to use you. He's going to work through you. And if you are His, He will even work out everything for your good. No amount of your disobedience is going to inconvenience His plan in the slightest!

But what kind of love story do you want to tell your children? And grandchildren? What do you want to be your testimony? Date accordingly.

Is Jesus Your Savior, or Just Your Imaginary Friend?

Honestly, the fear that strikes me when I meet someone who says they're pursuing Jesus, but they also want to pursue a dating relationship with someone who doesn't love Jesus, is this: they may not truly know Jesus.

Maybe they had a conversion experience where they walked down an aisle, made a profession of faith, or felt something truly special, but at the end of the day, it was more or less just that: an experience.

But Jesus never invites us into an experience. He invites us into a relationship! Jesus says, "Come and follow me." Not just on Sundays, or just at church camp, or just on a mission trip, or just down the street to run some errands. And not only when it feels good or easy. (Is it *ever* easy?)

Jesus's invitation is to follow Him every day of every week of every month of every year of your life. And to those who don't know Him, I can see how that sounds like some daunting sentence they have to serve.

However, that's where faith comes in, because as you follow Him by faith, one day at a time, you grow to know, believe, and depend on His love and grace like the air that fills your lungs and the gravity that keeps you grounded.

Do I still sin, despite my love for Jesus? Yes, absolutely, but I can't justify my sin. His love for me is so precious, I want to respond to it in obedience. I want to repent of my sin instead of rationalizing it.

Do you know Jesus like this?

Is Jesus even real to you? Is He really your Savior who wants to show you the path of life, or more like an imaginary friend who gives you the comfort only your imagination can give?

YOU MIGHT ALREADY KNOW "THE ONE"

Is the Jesus you claim to follow the God revealed in scripture who meets your deepest need for forgiveness and mercy? Or is He some God, defined by our culture, who will grant your every desire, if you're good enough?

In other words, is this the reality: you just *want* to believe in Jesus, like a kid wants to believe in Santa and the Easter Bunny? And if you do believe Jesus is your real and true friend, are you *His* real and true friend?

> *You are my friends if you do what I command you.*
> —John 15:14 ESV

Don't take that last verse as a guilt trip. It's just a statement of fact, not a threat. Jesus isn't saying, "If you don't do what I say, I won't be your friend anymore." He's saying, "I am your one true friend. And if you truly know my love, you'll trust me enough to do whatever I say."

Will you trust Him?

THE 10TH DATING COMMANDMENT

Dating Commandment #10: Thou shalt not rush the process you hope will lead you to a life-giving, lifelong marriage.

Do you find yourself attracted to any of these Mr./Ms. Wrongs? If so, hit pause and share your vulnerability with good friends and mentors. Talk through why you find one or more of these unhealthy personality profiles so enticing.

Do you always seem to attract the wrong person? If so, slow down and seek wise counsel to determine what's drawing these unhealthy people into your orbit. You probably need to change your social circle, your social cues, or both.

Do you *personally* identify with one of these unhealthy personality profiles? If so, now is not the time for your dating life to begin. However, working through your issues with solid friends and wise mentors can get you there in time. And in the meantime, you'll save yourself (and others) much heartache, rejection, and regret.

This chapter marks the end of the third lesson in an 8-week LoveEd study. For discussion questions and resources go to:

FMUniversity.net/DatePrep-wk3

CHAPTER 7:
ARE YOU GUILTY OF RELATIONAL MALPRACTICE?

Many believe the dating process is broken. As a result, different writers have proposed various courtship models where a suitor must step through a series of specific obligations before dating a particular young lady.

But what about your dating practices? You know, like how you carry yourself and treat your date?

Because whether you call it dating or courtship—whether you ask for parental blessing before the first date, before engagement, or never—many out there dating are doing it wrong. And they don't even know it! They only know they never seem to get to wherever it is they think they want to get to.

Are you not getting what you want out of dating? What if it isn't the process that's at fault, but the practices you've picked up from the media or older siblings or tales from family members "who just knew they were 'the one'" on the first date. Or *before* the first date?

Could you be guilty of relational malpractice? In this chapter and the three that follow, we will share four dating don'ts, common dating practices to avoid if you want to succeed in dating and enjoy the process.

DATING DON'T #1: DON'T DITCH YOUR FRIENDS

Friends are often your first go-to for sharing what's going on in your world.

Got an A? Got a promotion? Got a new car? Meet up with your party peeps and celebrate. Have a 500-page paper due? Lost the promotion to the coworker you can't stand? Totaled your new car? Meet up with your homies and vent.

After all, what are friends for?

Well, for many, once you're in a serious relationship, friends are for ditching.

Of course, if you've been dating someone for months and are seriously considering marriage, it's normal and healthy for your significant other to become your first go-to. And as you spend more and more time getting to know this creature of wonder, you're going to have less time for your friends.

However, let's be real, some people dump their friends after a first date. Or after the first all-night text-fest.

If that's you; if every time you get a boo you ghost your friends, you are not a good friend. So be honest. Is this your pattern in friendship and dating?

"I love you guys! What would I do without you?!"

The next day: "Oh you'll never guess who likes me! Bye!"

The next month: "Oh they were such a jerk! I can't believe I fell for them!! I love you guys! What would I do without you?!"

This person may appear to be changing their focus from their friends to their love interest and back to their friends, but in reality, their focus isn't changing at all. Instead, they're continually focused on themselves.

With that self focus, they look to their friends to encourage and validate them. Until they're "in a relationship" and then they look to their babe to encourage and validate them. Until the breakup, and then they're seeking their friends again.

BEHIND EVERY GREAT LOVER ARE GREAT FRIENDS

That said, ditching your friends whenever you get a lover isn't merely self-centered, it's self-destructive.

That's the irony of self-centeredness. It seems like you're looking out for your best interests—yourSELF—but you're actually grasping for your immediate gratification, not your long-term health. Which isn't in your best interest at all.

This is why, far from excluding your friends, you should be inviting them into your dating life. Those who know you best and love you most should know what's going on. In real time! They shouldn't hear about all the red flags and relational struggles you hid from them until after you've broken up and are brokenhearted.

Again, this pattern is at once both self-centered and self-destructive. You keep your friends from knowing the facts that could help them help you, and then when the truth finally comes out, you're a far bigger mess than you would have been if you had the wisdom and humility to be open and honest with them all along.

Your friends go from being dumped *by* you … to being dumped *on* by you … to being dumped *by* you again.

I'm not saying your best friends should tag along on every date, but I do think that in the early months of a dating relationship you should spend as much time hanging out with your significant other *along with* your friends as you spend on one-on-one dates.

Faithful, wise friends will observe things you can't see about yourself, your sweetie-weetie, and your relationship. Some of those things may be stuff you don't *want* to see at the time, but in the end, everyone wishes they would have known and acted on the truth.

Plus, not all the observations your friends make will be negative. Some may encourage you to pursue the relationship all the more, while other advice will enable you to make course corrections which may not only preserve but also strengthen your relationship.

In the end, nurturing, instead of abandoning, your closest and wisest friendships, will help you hone your relational skills of intimacy, intentionality, vulnerability, and honesty. All pro-skills for wise daters.

That's what friends are for!

I had friends like the ones I'm describing back when I was dating in college, and I can't imagine how differently my dating life might have gone without them in the thick of it with me.

I can't imagine how different my entire *life* would be without them. What follows is just one example of how God worked through these sorts of friendships to prepare me for a serious relationship and to guide me in my dating pursuits.

DO YOU WANT TO DATE WITH CONFIDENCE?

I lived with the same three guys my last three years at college. By God's grace, it seems we were good for each other.

One of the principles we stuck to through the three years we lived together was this one: pals before gals.

I'm aware that some guys may set that standard motivated by a misogynistic "he-man/woman-hater" mindset, while others might set that standard out of some kind of ultra-conservative, anti-dating perspective. But for me and my roommates? We all wanted to wind up with a girl. We just wanted to protect each other from winding up with the wrong girl.

We had fun with it too. If any one of us seemed to be hanging out with the same girl a little too frequently, the relentless teasing would commence. More constructively, we would pool our collective knowledge of those we were interested in to determine which young ladies were worth risking the heart of one of our beloved roommates.

Stuart, one of the four of us, even added a threat to the "pals before gals" mantra, warning us, "If any of you get a girlfriend, I'm going to kick your butt. With my cowboy boots on." And the rest of us knew he wasn't kidding. We knew that if we were going to get into a relationship that wasn't right, he cared enough about us to step in. With his boots on.

So when Julie and I started talking seriously about dating, I was more than a little nervous. And honestly? Not just because of Stuart, but because of one of my other roommates, Greg. Fact is, Julie and Greg had dated our freshman year, and it didn't work out.

However, this was two years later, and we had all grown. Plus, my relationship with Julie had grown a lot, and my pastor and accountability partners were all green-lighting it. But I dreaded telling my roommates.

I didn't know how they would react. Especially Greg (who had dated her) and Stuart (who had really big cowboy boots).

Then one afternoon, Fred (the other roommate who hadn't dated Julie or threatened me with his boots) asked me out of the clear blue, "Have you and Julie ever thought about becoming more than friends?"

I was totally taken off guard. I wish we could have recorded my reaction on video because I would like to hear how I awkwardly managed to stammer, "Ah … what? Julie? Ah … Julie? Why would you ask?"

"Well," Fred continued, "Stuart, Greg, and I were talking about how well-matched you and Julie seem to be. You get along so well together. And Greg mentioned that he hoped his past relationship with Julie wouldn't keep you from pursuing her."

I remember I was standing in our bedroom, which was on the bottom floor of a two-story apartment building, but I swear that the Shekinah glory of the Lord shone down from heaven and burst through the ceiling, as the Spirit of God descended like a dove right into the room.

Needless to say, I came clean with Fred. But I still had to reckon with the boots.

"You know what this means," Stuart remarked with a wicked grin, after he heard the news later that day.

So that night, I found myself sitting alone on the sofa in our living room in the dark as I waited for my roommates to come out in a solemn procession, two of them carrying candles that lit up the room enough for me to see Stuart's old boots. Not on his feet, but in his hands.

And he gave me that pair of boots that night. Instead of a kick in the butt, I got his blessing. I received *all* of their blessings.

My roommates joined my pastor and accountability partners in giving a thumbs-up to me pursuing a relationship with Julie. I had the approval of all the guys I was closest to, all the guys who knew me best and loved me most.

But it got better the next day when I left for class with my new boots on.

As soon as I opened my front door, I saw chalked out on the sidewalk in front of our apartment, "New boots, Mike?"

And then on the telephone pole in the parking lot, there was a poster stapled to it which read, "New boots, Mike?"

And so on, all across campus, my roommates (and probably other friends they had recruited) chalked the phrase on sidewalks and hung posters on light poles, bulletin boards, and bathroom walls.

"New boots, Mike?"

So by the end of the school day, everyone who knew us now knew Julie and I were dating seriously.

Wouldn't you like that kind of encouragement and support in your dating life?

Of course you would.

But you don't make friends like this by accident. You need to set out to pursue them with the same intentionality and intensity you would pursue a romantic relationship. Ah, but the dividends are priceless!

WISE COUNSEL MAKES THE DIFFERENCE IN DATING

Wiser decisions are always made with wise counsel. Logic not only tells us this. Scripture tells us this.

> *Or what king, going out to encounter another king in war, will not sit down first and deliberate whether he is able with ten thousand to meet him who comes against him with twenty thousand? And if not, while the other is yet a great way off, he sends a delegation and asks for terms of peace.* —Luke 14:31-32 ESV

How big a fool would a king have to be to set out to win a battle against an enemy twice his strength without first seeking wise counsel? A treacherous fool because his recklessness not only endangers his own life, but the lives of all his men, as well as the lives of all the citizens who rely on their king for protection!

Yet I see fools set out on the adventure of dating as if there were no risks involved. Not only refusing to consider how they could wound their own heart but how they could wound the hearts of those they date, as well as the hearts of those who care about them or those they date.

Meanwhile, other fools listen to fear instead of wise counsel. Not wishing to risk anything, they avoid dating altogether, like a king who won't resolve to either meet his enemy in battle or in peace negotiations. Refusing to put yourself out there may seem a smarter move than rushing into romance without a battle plan, but instead of getting shot down in your dating life, you'll likely trap yourself in lifelong singleness.

If you're going to date, you're going to risk. This is why you want wise counsel. A solid group of friends and mentors could not only boost your confidence but also equip you with strategies for preparing to date well.

> *A man of many companions may come to ruin, but there is a friend who sticks closer than a brother.* —Proverbs 18:24 ESV

YOU PROBABLY DON'T NEED MORE DATING EXPERIENCE

What is marriage really? Most of the time? Candlelit dinners and rolling in the deep between the sheets, every single day, for as long as you both shall live?

Of course not! It's sharing the mundane: cleaning the dishes, paying the bills, serving your community, and, for a season, it will largely be invested in raising your kids (if God so blesses). Oh, and most of your time together between the sheets will not be spent "sleeping together," but just sleeping.

Do you really think dating a bunch of different dating partners will help you prepare for all of that? Instead, doesn't this make more sense?

- If you want to prepare to be a great friend to your future spouse, learn to love your friends well.

- If you want to prepare to be a great roommate to your future spouse, learn to live in harmony with everyone you share a home with.

- If you want to prepare to be a great coworker with your future spouse, learn to serve well and lead well at every job you get.

- If you want to prepare to be a great team player with your future spouse, learn to communicate and cooperate on every team you're a part of.

- If you want to prepare to be a great parent with your future spouse, learn to set an example for the younger people who look up to you right now.

Dating isn't required for any of that! Friendships are!

FRIENDSHIP LOVE IS GREATER THAN ROMANTIC LOVE

Every Christian knows God's unconditional love ("agape" is the Greek word) is the ultimate love we need. But after God's love, which is stronger?

> A. Romantic/sexual love (what the Greeks call eros)
> B. Friendship/brotherly love (what the Greeks call phileo)

I hold that most believe romantic love is the ultimate love our soul craves. Our culture veritably screams out, "Give me eros or give me death!"

Even in the church, where marriage is promoted as the only relationship where sex is celebrated, the misguided assumption is that romantic/sexual love must be the bomb dot com, while friendship love is kinda just for kids before their hormones kick in and their eyes are opened.

But here's the surprising truth: it is *not* romantic/sexual love that ultimately makes a marriage work. Instead, after your faithful attempts at extending agape love toward your future spouse, it will be plain ol' brotherly love that will hold your marriage together.

In fact, a married couple sharing no deep friendship will, over time, find their sex life empty and hollow. That is if they still have a sex life at all. Please believe me, I know many men in marriages like this. There is no friendship, so there is no sex. None. At. All.

So you see, a great marriage is not so much an epic romance as it is a faithful friendship, a faithful friendship that may very well foster an epic romance, but the friendship is the core, the essential ingredient.

STOP IDOLIZING ROMANCE

Admittedly, romantic/sexual love is pretty dang powerful. It's like dynamite.

But close friendship—brotherly love—is also powerful but less flashy, like cement and steel.

Dynamite is fun and exciting, but you can't build much with it. In the same way, eros love is electric and intoxicating, but you can't build on it. Maybe, like dynamite, it can clear the ground for building the foundation of a relationship, but you can't use romance or sex to actually build a foundation.

So stop idolizing romance, and learn to treasure, seek, and build strong friendships before you seek to build a dating relationship. Then use the same relational skills you honed in your best friendships to build a foundation for your dating life and every one of your dating relationships.

CHAPTER 8:

YOU GET WHAT YOU PREPARE FOR

When it comes to looking for the right job, most will go to a lot of work to prepare for the interview process: researching potential employers and their respective openings, honing interview skills, and dressing for success. And the higher the position you're going for, the greater the effort you'll want to put into preparation.

In contrast, most folks show up to a first date with almost no thought of preparation beyond dressing to slay.

However, if you're looking for a future spouse, you ultimately need one person to fill the following roles in your life, as you fill the same roles in their life:

- Best friend
- Roommate
- Financial partner
- Sexual companion
- Team player
- Co-parent of your children

Oh, and don't forget that you're looking to make a lifetime appointment.

Don't you think your dating practices should measure up? Then you want to internalize this next dating don't, which will require some date prep on your part.

DATING DON'T #2: DON'T KILL THE CONVERSATION

You really want to get to know your date better? Then what needs to happen to succeed in this endeavor?

You have to talk! You have to carry on a conversation. And then another one. And another. So commit to dating practices which enable you to do that so you can find out if you truly enjoy, understand, and respect each other.

MOVIES: DATE WITHOUT THEM, BUT TALK ABOUT THEM

I'm not downing "dinner and a movie" because it's cliché. First, I'm not downing dinner at all, and second, I love movies! My first date with the girl who became my wife was to see the motion picture classic, *Teenage Mutant Ninja Turtles*. (Kowabunga, dude!)

However, what is the one thing you are forbidden by the laws of society from doing during a movie?

Talking!

So if the point of dating involves getting to know your date better, how does spending half your dating life sitting next to each other in the dark without sharing a word help you accomplish this objective? It doesn't.

I don't want to criminalize movies on dates. I just want to discourage them, especially early in a dating relationship, including every first date. YES! I just confessed to watching a movie on a first date with my now-wife, but I couldn't read this book back then. Because it hadn't yet been written. And in the end, very little of our dating life involved movies.

If you must watch a movie on a date, at least switch it up, and do the movie first and then dinner. That way you get a whole mealtime to talk about what you just watched, what you liked, didn't like, and why.

Even better? Talk about the movies you love. You can learn so much about a person from their media intake, including the following:

- Whether they view movies more as a tool to escape life or to understand life

- What aspects of the movies they appreciate most, least, or not at all, and why (dialogue, plot, acting, cinematography, special effects, story, themes, ideas, or messages)

- What makes them laugh or cry

- What makes them uncomfortable or angry

- Who they want to emulate and who they can't stand

- What offends them or scares them and what doesn't

- How strong their convictions are about various behaviors, language, and lifestyles and how their convictions shape their movie-watching choices

- How their movie-watching choices shape their convictions as well as shape the way they view themselves, others, God, and life in general

FEELING CLOSER IS NOT THE SAME AS GROWING CLOSER

Movies, concerts, television … There are infinite entertainment options that can kill the conversation in your dating life by limiting or even preventing dialogue.

Of course, getting tickets to see their favorite artist together demonstrates you care about them. It also provides a fun way to connect and unforgettable memories. However, those memories won't be of what you learned about each other. They'll be about the experience you shared.

You might think, "So what? We'll be making memories." Well, this leads us to an important truth you need to grasp if you want to date in a healthy and whole way.

Psychology reveals that shared experiences have a way of making people feel closer, whether the shared experience is an entertaining event like a movie or concert, or a traumatic event like an accident or hostage situation.

But feeling closer and actually growing closer are not the same thing. We can walk away feeling closer after watching a movie or concert without any of the intentionality, vulnerability, understanding, or effort necessary to actually grow closer through intimate conversation.

So if you want to truly get to know your date, you need to be sharing personal stories, opinions, values, aspirations, not just sharing experiences.

PUT DOWN THE PHONE AND DATE!

Never before the smartphone could two people sit across from one another for an hour or more and never share a word without it being awkward.

Sadly, this is why the smartphone has become the distraction of choice. It somehow alleviates us from ever feeling (or looking) awkward, lonely, listless, or unimportant.

In the olden days before phones were in our pockets, the world was filled with the potential for conversation. Today, the smartphone has all but killed those potential conversations. It has become such a crutch for many that it can eliminate a lot of opportunities for great dating dialogue.

- Awkward lull in a conversation? Just look at your phone!

- Feeling anxious? Just look at your phone!

- Offended by something they said? Just look at your phone …
  then let out a gasp and apologetically explain you had
  forgotten you have to be somewhere else right then
  because your phone just reminded you.

Again, you can use the phone to generate conversation. I know this. I've *done* this. You share texts, memes, videos, social media posts, but eventually you should be leaning on your own ideas instead of those of your favorite social media account. And so should your date.

WHAT YOU CAN LEARN FROM FLIRTING WITH SOMEONE

All conversations are *not* created equal. In other words, you can share very deeply and meaningfully with someone you're close to with a short text, or you can spend all night talking with someone and never really learn much about them at all.

In fact, one pervasive dating practice can keep two people chatting it up for an hour or more. And having a great time! And yet never saying anything of import.

I'm talking about the age-old practice of flirting.

To clarify, I'm not discouraging mature efforts to convey sincere interest in someone else. Nothing is wrong with that when done purposefully and prudently, but that's *not* what flirting is by definition.

In fact, by definition, it's the opposite of flirting. Merriam-Webster defines flirting as "to behave amorously **without serious intent**," or "to show

superficial or **casual** interest or liking."[3] In a sense, flirting is like relational candy. So enjoyable, and at the same time, so empty.

However, if the goal of flirting is to demonstrate interest in another as you gauge their interest in return, you would think that at the very least two people who spent an hour or so flirting would know whether they like each other. But do they?

Remember, flirting is insincere. By definition, it has "no serious intent"; it's "superficial." So while one person will flirt with you because they like you, another will flirt with you simply because they like to flirt. And you just so happened to be available.

Still, others flirt, not because they like *you*, but because they like *themselves* and want attention. They know they have the looks or sensual qualities others admire, and they enjoy using these to their advantage. Finally, some flirt because they *don't* like themselves and are seeking affirmation. They have huge insecurities about their appearance or sex appeal, and they put on a bold front to mask their self-doubt.

Regardless of the motive, whether you spend all evening at a party flirting with whoever will give you the time of night or whether you save all your flirting for that one person you've had your eye on for the last four months, when the evening is over, what have you truly learned about the other person? And what have they learned about you?

WHY WE FLIRT

I suppose I believed flirting would help me find my spouse. You know, like I would flirt with her. And she with me. And then we would be married in the morning! Or maybe at least kiss.

---

[3] *"Flirting Definition & Meaning,"* Merriam-Webster (Merriam-Webster), accessed May 20, 2022, https://www.merriam-webster.com/dictionary/flirting.

Since I flirted with every single attractive girl I ever met back then (even if they weren't single), that included the girl I eventually did marry. So I guess you could say it worked, right?

However, while Julie and I *did* flirt back when we first met, I can't say flirting played a key role in building our relationship. In fact, instead of advancing our relationship, in many ways, it stunted it.

Since those days, I've done quite a bit of thinking about why I flirted so much and have come up with two more honest answers, one that was pretty obvious and one that wasn't.

The obvious answer to why I flirted? It was fun! Flirting allowed my quick wit, dry sarcasm, and comic timing to shine. And it felt good to get a girl's attention and keep her attention. Even better if I made her laugh and kept her laughing.

The nonobvious answer to why I flirted? It was safe. Because when I was flirting, I was more or less acting. I wasn't playing the sort-of-sad-but-true role of the guy who had never had a girlfriend in his life. I was playing the fun, light-hearted role of the lady's man, who could have a girlfriend if he'd only be willing to settle down.

But bottom line, if my flirting was well received, if I offered an over-the-top compliment and they returned with an over-the-top response like, "finally somebody gets me," then we could have some fun.

On the other hand, if my flirting was rejected, if I played some bad pickup line and was firmly put in my place, it wasn't really me who was being rejected. It was the role I was playing.

Can you relate at all?

If so, leave the acting for the movies, and just say "no" to flirting.

HOW TO SHARE EXPERIENCES AND CONVERSATION AT THE SAME TIME

Though you don't want to kill the conversation in your dating life, you shouldn't feel like you have to talk all the time.

I get it! It can be stressful, especially on a first date. Simply sharing a cup of coffee can lead to a panic attack, especially if one or both of you are introverts.

So, here are some dating ideas to enable you to share fun experiences and meaningful conversation at the same time.

Play together:

- Attend a sporting event (unlike movies, concerts, or live theater, most sporting events give you plenty of breaks for conversation).

- Walk, hike, run, bike, skateboard, scooter, kayak, canoe, or boat.

- Enjoy outdoor games like frisbee, disc golf, corn hole, or mini golf.

- Go to a community event like an art crawl or festival.

Learn together:

- Walk through a museum of art, history, or science.

- Cook a meal together or build something together.

- Sign up for a lesson in pottery, ballroom dancing, glassblowing, or painting.

Serve together:

- Visit a residential care facility, homeless shelter, or soup kitchen.

- Do yard work for a shut-in or clean up a park.

- Work at the local animal shelter.

Each of the above experiences not only allows ample space for casual, yet meaningful, dialogue, it provides opportunities to interact with your date in ways that could be unique, memorable, insightful, and character-revealing.

In addition to keeping your dating life fresh and vibrant, interacting with your date in diverse environments as you engage in various activities allows you to better discern their interests, values, character, and your chemistry working or playing together. Or not.

So go forth and date with dialogue!

CHAPTER 9:
WHO ARE YOU GOING TO TRUST WITH YOUR HEART?

As long as we're talking about relational malpractice, let's use an analogy from the medical realm, where malpractice is also a pretty big deal. Imagine you needed serious heart surgery. Who would you want to carry out the procedure?

A. A brand-new surgeon fresh out of their residency
B. The most gorgeous heart surgeon you can find on the internet
C. A world-renowned heart surgeon with 20 years of experience
D. Your mom

A rhetorical question, right? If someone is going to cut you open and mess around with your heart, the only criterion that matters is their preparedness to do so carefully and successfully.

Yet when it comes to dating, our criterion usually has nothing to do with how prepared someone is to handle our heart. Instead, we'll settle for anyone we're physically attracted to who will give us their heart as well. Can you see why dating so often turns out so badly?

So, keep that in mind as you consider these four dating don'ts. They're not intended to keep you from having fun but to keep you from damaging your heart or the hearts of those you date.

DATING DON'T #3: DON'T COMPROMISE YOUR CONVICTIONS

Do you have any convictions? I'm not talking about your criminal record. I'm talking about principles you live and die by.

If you do, then don't engage in dating practices which will make it more difficult (or even impossible) to honor your convictions.

I'm not talking about boundaries either. Boundaries are what you set to honor your convictions. Convictions are the "why" behind your boundaries.

And if you don't know your convictions? You need to put your dating life on hold and figure out what your convictions are first. (We talk more about them in Chapter 19.)

Bottom line, a mature adult (which is the only type of person who's ready to date) should meet the following standards:

- Know and honor their convictions
- Make their convictions clear to their date
- Insist their date honor their convictions
- Know and honor their date's convictions in return

In fact, your convictions are so important, it demands you avoid dating practices that endanger them.

NO DATE SHOULD BE WORTH MORE THAN YOUR CONVICTIONS

What's the big deal with compromising your convictions, if it might mean winning (or keeping) the love of your life?

For starters, though tradeoffs abound in every part of life, convictions aren't supposed to be disposable or even malleable. They're designed to be foundational. In other words, instead of letting the people you date determine which convictions you'll hold onto or not, your convictions are supposed to determine which people you will date or not.

Secondly, it's important to note that your convictions seldom just come to you out of nowhere. They usually come to you through your most important relationships in life: family, church, or directly from God.

This means you can't alter your convictions without impacting those relationships. You should think long and hard about making significant compromises to keep or grow a relationship with someone you just met, or have known even a couple of years, no matter how fine a specimen of humanity.

Bottom line, a person with no firm convictions lacks an understanding of who they are and to whom they belong. This means that if they let their dating life determine their convictions, instead of the other way around, then their identity will be defined by their dating relationships.

WHAT IF YOUR CONVICTIONS ARE WRONG?

How do you know if you have the right convictions?

Perhaps you'll only watch G movies. (So that only leaves certain animated movies and live action movies prior to 1960.) Or maybe you're saving your first kiss for your tenth wedding anniversary. (If that's so, I hope it's with your spouse.)

What if you're being too legalistic? What if there's pride instead of humility behind the boundaries you set for yourself? Or what if your convictions are motivated more by the fear of messing up or angering God than by your love for God and your desire to please Him?

All fair questions! Questions you want to discuss with good friends and mentors who are older in the faith and wiser in experience, not with someone you're falling in love with and would be open to changing almost anything for.

Admittedly, in the end, your identity is going to be powerfully changed by the person you wind up marrying. That's part of what it means to become one flesh. It would then logically follow that your identity is probably going to adapt as you're dating that person you feel led to marry. But in a healthy individual, all of these adjustments should strengthen the convictions you have inherited from those who know you best and love you most. Not deconstruct them.

WHAT TO DO WHEN THEY PUSH YOUR BOUNDARIES

Here's the deal. If you know your convictions, you know at least two essential things about yourself:

1. You know who you are (because your convictions define you).

2. You know who you belong to (because you always derive and share convictions with those who are important to you).

So if someone doesn't honor your convictions, you know at least two essential things about them:

1. They want to change who you are (defining you by their own convictions, or lack thereof).

2. They want to change who you belong to. (But a healthy dating relationship shouldn't ask you to leave behind those who know and love you best.)

So why would you accept someone who seems intent on violating your convictions? Or even someone who is condescending toward them? Can you see how that person isn't the one for you?

Yes, even if they're really good looking, really fun, and really sweet in so many other ways. Yes, even if they feel the same way about you.

Look! I get it! I know falling for someone who falls for you in return doesn't exactly happen every day. (At least it didn't for me.)

Further, I know many fantastic single folks who haven't had a serious romance in a decade. Or more. Or ever! And I can understand how the pressure to surrender certain convictions in order to secure a spouse could feel overwhelming.

But I also know many folks who felt that same pressure to compromise their standards to get their spouse and—congratulations—they did and they did. They made the compromises, and they got their spouse.

And years later they feel stuck with them. Until death. Or until divorce. If they aren't divorced already.

Someone who truly loves you will honor your convictions. They will! A person who truly loves you will honor the person your convictions have made you and will honor the important people in your life who helped you form those convictions.

HOW MANY CHANCES SHOULD YOU GIVE YOUR DATE?

The longer a healthy relationship continues, the more casual and unguarded you will become. This is a good thing, because the "real you" is coming out. You shouldn't have to perform in meaningful relationships.

All of that said, if your date is already challenging your convictions on a first date or even in the first couple months of a dating relationship, you must recognize they are doing this even as they are on their best behavior.

Likewise, if the person you're dating doesn't start pushing your boundaries until later in the relationship, keep in mind, they're merely beginning to show you more of who they really are. And, trust me, as disappointing as that may be in this instance, it's better to know sooner rather than later.

So, how many times do you think you should tolerate a little boundary-pushing? That's a question you should wrestle with in light of the facts shared here and the counsel of those who know you best and love you most.

And how many times should you compromise your convictions? How about never.

WHAT IF YOU'RE ABLE TO GET AWAY WITH IT?

Of course, whenever Satan tempts us, he's always promising we'll escape the consequences of our actions.

> *But the serpent said to the woman, "You will not surely die."*
> —Genesis 3:4 ESV

But commonly, we *don't* get away with it. Not forever.

Truth has a way of catching up with us, even when we think we've given ourselves a huge head start. I guess you could say Truth is a pretty stellar long-distance runner.

However, sometimes we do get away with it!

Maybe that will be you.

But allow me to share the story of someone who *did* get away with compromising their convictions, specifically in the area of sexual sin.

The story comes from the movie, *Quiz Show*, but you don't have to know a thing about the film to learn from this brief exchange.

> **Dick Goodwin:** *You know, I remember five, six years ago my Uncle Harold told my aunt about this affair he had. It was a sort of mildly upsetting event in my family.*

Charles Van Doren: *Mm-hmm. Mildly?*

Dick Goodwin: *Well, you have to put it in context. See, the thing of it is, the affair was over somethin' like eight years ago.* (In other words, this affair had ended eight years before his uncle ever confessed.)

So, I remember askin' him, "Well, why'd you tell her? You got away with it." And I'll never forget what he said.

It was the "getting away with it" part he couldn't live with.[4]

What if you do wind up in a fantastic marriage with a fantastic spouse, parenting fantastic kids, and no one ever learns of your previous dating dalliances?

Might you wind up feeling like Dick Goodwin's uncle? Maybe the "getting away with it" part will be something you can't live with.

[4] *"Movie Scripts,"* Quiz Show (1994) Movie Scripts | SQ, accessed May 20, 2022, https://www.stockq.org/moviescript/Q/quiz-show.php.

CHAPTER 10:

THE CHAPTER THAT'S ALL ABOUT SEX

In this "sexclusive" chapter, we will not only share our final dating don't, we'll share its corollary, which is actually the secret to whoops-proofing your dating life. But let's begin with a word picture that clarifies why so many sweet (and even spiritually strong) Christian couples wind up falling into sexual sin so easily.

BODY ODOR & SEXUAL SIN

Imagine you had a significant issue with body odor. An issue so serious you applied copious amounts of antiperspirant before every date. With a spatula. And even that was futile.

If this was your reality (play along with me here), do you think you would engage in frequent, strenuous physical activities on dates guaranteed to get you perspiring? Or would you enjoy one-on-one time with your date in the heat of day inside a parked car with the AC off?

Why would you do such things if you know you'll end up sweating like a pig as you secrete a stench strong enough to repel a rabid skunk?

Wouldn't you want to keep your body temperature and heart rate low, if not out of self-respect, then out of honor for your date, who would be forced to tolerate your natural scent of death? Of course you would!

Yet two sincere Christians, who know sexual temptation is a reality, will nevertheless frequently engage in sexually arousing activities that get their body temperature rising and heart racing.

- They'll watch entertainment featuring gratuitous sexual situations and dialogue that mocks sexual purity.

- They'll dress in such a way as to say, "Dinner is served!"

- They'll flirt with each other using sexual inuendo.

- They'll engage in a kiss-fest that gets at least one of their sexual engines running in the red.

- They'll enjoy one-on-one time with their date in the heat of the night, inside a parked car with no one around.

And some will even do all of the above, date after date, and feel a certain pride about "not going too far," even boasting about holding onto their virginity card.

Then, if and when they do fall into sexual sin, they'll be more or less shocked, saying things like, "it just happened," or "we just fell into it," or "we just lost control." The word "just" serving to communicate that there were no preceding events or behaviors that could have predicted the sin that followed.

So, if you are committed to saving sex for the covenant relationship of marriage, refuse to engage in sexually arousing activities that get your engine running in overdrive. Save all that for the marriage bed too. *All* of it.

STAYING SEXUALLY PURE REQUIRES LOGIC. NOT LEGALISM!

I'm not saying that since you shouldn't have sex then you shouldn't make out, and if you shouldn't make out then you shouldn't touch, and if you shouldn't touch then you shouldn't even look at your date.

I'm not saying any of that!

If wrestling on a sofa together lip-locked for thirty minutes leaves neither of you turned on sexually, then, congratulations, you haven't sinned! But if the reality is that your dating practices necessitate a cool down or release afterward, you are flirting with danger.

Because if you want to avoid a certain sin, you need to avoid moving toward that sin. This isn't legalism. This is logic.

The writer of Proverbs 7 makes the case:

> *For at the window of my house I have looked out through my lattice, and I have seen among the simple, I have perceived among the youths, a young man lacking sense, passing along the street near her corner, taking the road to her house in the twilight, in the evening, at the time of night and darkness. And behold, the woman meets him, dressed as a prostitute, wily of heart.* —Proverbs 7:6-10 ESV

The principle here? If you move toward sin, expect sin to meet you.

And notice the writer says, "I have perceived … a young man lacking *sense.*" He doesn't say, "I have perceived a young man lacking righteousness or holiness or goodness or godliness."

He doesn't make a *moral* judgment. He makes a *rational* judgment. "I saw this dude heading toward sin, like he didn't know where it would lead him! Crazy, right?"

STOP SINNING AT ITS BEGINNING

Where does sin start? Jesus hints at that in His sermon on the mount.

> *You have heard that it was said, "You shall not commit adultery."*
> *But I say to you that everyone who looks at a woman with lustful*
> *intent has already committed adultery with her in his heart.*
> —Matthew 5:27-28 ESV

There's no way around Jesus's words in Matthew 5. If you're even thinking about sexual sin, it is as if you've already committed the sin of adultery in your heart.

Yes, even if you're not married. Yes, even if the person you're lusting over isn't married. Jesus doesn't specify the marital status of the one lusting or the one being lusted after.

But *why* did Jesus say this? Is Jesus trying to add to the burden of the law?

No! He's merely pointing out what we often lose sight of. Sin always starts in the mind.

Remember the dude in the previous passage from Proverbs 7, heading down the wrong street? Can't you hear him thinking to himself before he ever set out, "Wouldn't it be amazing to see her again … I wonder if she's busy tonight?"

Sin doesn't start when we start sinning. Sin starts when we start *thinking* about sinning. Sin doesn't spring out of thin air. It springs out of desire.

> *Let no one say when he is tempted, "I am being tempted by God,"*
> *for God cannot be tempted with evil, and he himself tempts no one.*
> *But each person is tempted when he is lured and enticed by his own*
> *desire.* **Then desire when it has conceived gives birth to sin, and**
> **sin when it is fully grown brings forth death.** —James 1:13-15
> ESV (emphasis mine)

So the battle for sexual purity, and for that matter, sexual wholeness, begins in the mind.

THE GOAL OF SEXUAL PURITY IS FREEDOM FROM SEXUAL SIN

We all want freedom from the consequences of sin, and Christ's blood does indeed free us from sin's *ultimate* consequence: eternal death. But God wants something far greater for us than freedom from the consequences of sin. He wants our freedom from sin itself.

Truthfully, what most of us would prefer is not freedom from sin but from temptation. We feel like if all temptation were removed, all sin would cease. That might be true, but would we be better for it? We wouldn't be sinning, but we would still be the sort of people who would sin if tempted to do so.

What if God isn't so interested in sin-free creatures, but creatures who can *resist* sin? A people who can triumph *over* sin!

This is why Christ not only died for our sin but also rose again. When it comes to sexual sin, God wants to empower us to master our sex drive, instead of being mastered by it.

> *All things are permitted for me, but not all things are of benefit.*
> *All things are permitted for me, but I will not be mastered*
> *by anything.* —1 Cor 6:12 NASB

But you can't be free of sexual sin when lust and sexual fantasy dominate your mind. So, if the goal of sexual purity is freedom from sexual sin, then there are two main disciplines we need to master:

1. Learning to avoid sexual temptation
2. Learning to resist sexual temptation

Avoiding sexually arousing dating practices will help you do both.

SEXUAL AROUSAL IS NATURAL AND GOOD!

Just because something (like sexual arousal) is natural and good doesn't mean it should be regarded as cheap or ordinary. Yet that is exactly how our culture treats sex.

In contrast, in Biblical marriage, sexual arousal is meant to be both extraordinary and essential! One thing is supposed to lead to another, and another, until there is nothing else to do except enjoy the afterglow. Only a good God would create something so special for couples committed for life to enjoy.

But you can't enjoy the afterglow of sin. Sin only leaves shame in its wake. Even though sexual arousal is natural and good, it was never meant to be treated like a mere recreational activity. It was meant to be treated like a reverent activity. And by "reverent" I don't mean quiet and solemn. I mean holy and intimate. A divine delight, if you will.

So date as if sexual arousal was normal, as if it were only natural to want to keep going and going and going until you were gone. Then establish boundaries and date accordingly.

DATING DON'T #4: DON'T ISOLATE!

Sexual arousal is normal, so set wise boundaries.

Sounds easy, right? Got it! Check!

Except for the fact that Satan isn't all that lazy when it comes to sexual temptation. In fact, he's coming after you. Not just to mess with you, or even rough you up, but to eat you for lunch.

> *Be sober-minded; be watchful. Your adversary the devil prowls*
> *around like a roaring lion, seeking someone to devour.*
> —1 Peter 5:8 ESV

THE CHAPTER THAT'S ALL ABOUT SEX

But there is one simple—not easy, but simple—way to almost guarantee success in your fight against sexual temptation on every date.

When you date, don't isolate. In other words, never put yourself and your date in a position where other people are not able to see you or walk in on you at any moment without warning. In fact, don't even take your date anywhere you don't *expect* to be seen often and without notice.

This means not dating in the following spaces:

- Rooms by yourself with the blinds shut and doors closed

- Buildings (including your homes) where no one else is present, awake, and within earshot and/or line of sight at all times

- Secluded places outdoors including parked cars

- Dark spaces indoors where you can't be seen

ONE SINGLE SEX BOUNDARY TO WHOOPS-PROOF YOUR DATING LIFE!

So if you refuse to isolate when you date, what are you going to do instead? That is the corollary to our final dating don't.

Keep your dating life out in the open.

This is the secret to whoops-proofing your dating life. I am aware this concept of refusing to isolate runs counter to what we consider totally normal in the realm of dating today, perhaps even the defining characteristic of modern dating. Indeed, spending endless hours alone talking or making out (or both) is celebrated in practically every coming-of-age story known to man (or woman) since the '60s.

It's assumed that high school students are going to hang out with their significant other in bedrooms (with the door closed) and parked cars (with the windows fogged). What's weird about that? Even "family friendly" movies display this behavior, only without nudity and cutting away before anything too serious happens.

It's a given that young adults are going to hang out with their significant other at each other's homes. What else are homes for? Are they not young *adults*?

This cultural reality makes keeping your dating life out in the open seem awkward and inconvenient at best, repressive or legalistic at worst. However, if you'll commit to this one boundary, I think you will find every awkward inconvenience worth it in the end when your dating days are done. In the meantime, you get to enjoy a dating life largely free from sexual tension and regret.

Dating in isolation may be normal now, but so is hooking up and cohabitation. And just how well is "normal" working out for our culture today? After all, throughout time people have successfully met and grown in relationship with their future spouse without extended times of private isolation. True story.

Beyond historical evidence, there are four different reasons why this one single sex boundary is so whoops-proof.

1. It eliminates the opportunity for sexual sin.
2. It works with the nature of sexual temptation.
3. It keeps you from reprogramming your sex drive.
4. It allows you to focus on relational intimacy.

TIRED OF FIGHTING SEXUAL TEMPTATION?

I don't know about you, but Julie and I found fighting sexual temptation wearying, especially the eleven months of our engagement. Honestly, sometimes we didn't even *want* to fight it.

Yet, time and time again, we'd put ourselves in positions where we *had* to fight sexual temptation. We'd go to one of our apartments when our roommates were out. Or we'd park some place and talk. And we *would* talk. At *first*. Or we would find an empty classroom to study in together. And we *would* study together. At *first*.

But bottom line, even if we were able to successfully fight temptation as much as half the time we isolated ourselves—or even 80% of the time—we would have never failed at all if we had refused to put ourselves in so many compromising situations.

We set (and then crossed) so many boundaries, but simply keeping our dating life out in the open would have eliminated the need for those other boundaries.

So here's **Purity Pro Tip #1: If you don't want to fight, don't get in the ring.** Spend more time *avoiding* sexual temptation and you'll spend less time having to *fight* it.

KILL SEXUAL FANTASY

Another reason keeping your dating life out in the open succeeds where other boundaries fail is because it works with the nature of sexual temptation. Remember, all temptation begins in the mind.

As a personal example, when I was dating Julie, I would anticipate an upcoming date by thinking, "First we're going to go get pizza and then since her roommates are out of town we'll go back to her place and talk … and then …" I'd start fantasizing about what we might do.

Of course, I'd also determine ahead of time we weren't going to do any of that. We were going to be strong this time. We were going to stick to the boundaries we had agreed to. But still I knew the date would end with us alone.

We call this an "on-ramp" to sexual sin. You can't get on the highway without an on-ramp, and contrarily, once you get on an on-ramp, turning around is incredibly difficult. The same reality comes into play with sexual sin. People act like sexual sin surprises them, when they've often fantasized about it numerous times before it ever happened.

Purity Pro Tip #2: If you don't want to go there, don't build an on-ramp. Eliminate the on-ramp, and you eliminate the starting point of another sexual fantasy.

This alone won't eliminate your struggle with sexual fantasy, but over time, it will help you win that battle too because our minds and bodies work together, either to lead us toward greater righteousness or toward greater sin.

So, every time your date ends without falling into sexual sin—even better, every time your date ends without getting you all sexually frustrated—the less material your mind has to work with for your next fantasy. Make sense?

SHOULD YOU REPROGRAM YOUR SEX DRIVE?

Almost nothing shocks me anymore, but certain things still manage to mystify me. Like Christian couples who move in together before marriage, yet with the intention of remaining abstinent until their wedding night.

How does that work? Is it like a middle school sleepover? Do you eat lots of candy and tell ghost stories? Or do you pretend you're just roommates? Roommates looking forward to a magical ceremony which will break the "just roommates" spell over your hearts and turn you into wild, passionate lovers?

Then there are more conservative, Bible-believing couples who would never consider cohabitating, yet who nevertheless endeavor to discipline themselves to spend countless hours alone together without getting into trouble.

As for me and Julie, once we were finally engaged, if we were alone together for an hour, or even thirty minutes, it was a battle to keep our hands to ourselves. And not because we wanted to wrestle like we were at a childhood sleepover.

I realize all sex drives are not created equal, but ignoring the issue of willpower, do you think intentionally testing your resolve on a regular basis is a good idea?

Remember, when two frisky love kittens are alone together, it is only natural for stuff to happen! Which means consistently resisting or suppressing sexual desire requires that you essentially reprogram your sex drive.

Is this what God is asking of "good little Christian daters"?

Beware: If You "Flip the Switch," You'll Have to Flip It Back

The sad reality is that most Christian dating couples who do manage to maintain sexual purity, despite spending countless hours alone together, wind up feeling like all their self-control is rewarded with incredible frustration in their marital sex life. (Not exactly the reward they were looking for.)

The common phrase you'll hear is that they aren't able to "flip the switch" after the wedding. Once they can finally say "YES" to sex, their bodies still seem set on saying, "NO!" In other words, their marriage vows turn out not to be magic words which turn them into wild, passionate lovers.

As a result, many of these formerly conservative, Christian dating couples are really bitter about it. Some of them are divorced. They claim "purity culture" taught them sex was bad, so even after marriage it still felt bad.

However, what they don't realize is they had already "flipped that switch" earlier, back when they were dating. All that time they spent alone together with the person they wanted to marry, they were disciplining themselves to suppress their natural biological sex instinct. Essentially, they were reprogramming their sex drive.

Again, sexual discipline is a good thing! Indeed, it's demanded of every follower of Christ. But after months of training their bodies to shut down sexually whenever they were alone together, they succeeded in flipping the switch of their sex drive. That is, flipping it to the "sexual arousal is naughty" setting.

After conditioning their minds to disassociate from their feelings when aroused by the person they planned to marry, they somehow expect that switch to be easy to flip back to the "sexual arousal is natural" setting when they can finally enjoy sex, sans guilt. However, it turns out it isn't easy. Definitely possible, but frustratingly difficult and complicated at first. And maybe for years.

But if you will stick to this one single sex boundary—keep your dating life out in the open—you won't have to reprogram your sex drive.

Purity Pro Tip #3: If you don't want to flip the switch, then don't flip the switch. In other words, if you don't want to have to "flip the switch" after marriage, then don't "flip the switch" before marriage. Treat sexual arousal like it's only natural between two lovers who want to be married, and date accordingly.

DISPENSE WITH THE DATING DISTRACTIONS

When I'm exercising, I will often pray. When I'm cycling, this can be a focused and meaningful time of prayer. However, when I'm running, this can be a frustrating and meaningless time of prayer.

Because when I'm running, I am often struggling just to breathe. I go from a prayer request to an "air request." Then I can be praising God for who He is and that I'm alive. Barely. Even though I feel like I'm dying. Am I dying? Breathe! Breathe! (You get the idea.)

All of that to say, the continuous exertion of strenuous exercise hinders my ability to focus on the person I'm trying to talk to, namely God.

What does this have to do with keeping your dating life out in the open?

Simply that when Julie and I isolated, a similar phenomenon would take place. I didn't have difficulty breathing, but I would spend an enormous amount of energy just struggling to keep my hands to myself. I would go from asking about her day to thinking how gorgeous she was, particularly in that moment. I would fight all the thoughts of what we could do together right then until I remembered the shame from the last time we messed around. Then I would wonder when her roommates were coming home.

In hindsight, all that tension was exhausting because my mind was divided. Part of me wanted to get to know Julie. The other part of me just wanted to get busy.

Scripture talks about not being double-minded. And not in a good way.

> *If any of you lacks wisdom, let him ask God, who gives generously to all without reproach, and it will be given him. But let him ask in faith, with no doubting, for the one who doubts is like a wave of the sea that is driven and tossed by the wind. For that person must not suppose that he will receive anything from the Lord; he is a double-minded man, unstable in all his ways.* —James 1:5-8 ESV

I could certainly relate to that wave of the sea, literally driven by the winds of my passion and lust. Can you?

Pro-tip #4: If you don't want to be driven by passion, don't divide your mind. Keep your dating life focused on the things that *will* matter if you wind up marrying. Not how well you make out, but how well you encourage, enjoy, understand, strengthen, and respect each other.

DON'T LET OUR SIN EXCUSE YOURS

You might be tempted to think, "Well, Julie and MJ turned out alright in the end." But you must remember, by God's grace, we invested over two years growing a stellar friendship before we even started to think about dating seriously.

However, what if you don't have any of that time to grow your friendship before you become serious? What if you meet, date, and fall in love all rather quickly without getting a couple years to truly get to know one another?

Then if your dating life is defined by sexual desire (whether giving in, fighting it, or both), you miss all that time and energy you could have been growing a friendship. This is the story of many, where sexual struggle more or less defines the majority of their relationship prior to marriage.

But even if you do get a couple years of friendship before the fireworks start, do you think we're suggesting this one single sex boundary to steal your joy?

To the contrary! We want to heighten your joy and save you the sexual frustration that we endured over the first seven to ten years of our married life because we did give into sin time and time again. Remember the law of the harvest is real!

DATE WITHOUT FEAR!

The first chapter of this book pointed out why contemporary dating fails so often. Then the following chapters identified ten dumb reasons to date, nine Mr./Ms. Wrongs, and four dating don'ts.

Dumb? Wrong? Don't? Why all the negatives? Because most won't be motivated to date differently until they fully grasp not only why the world's pattern doesn't work, but all the various ways the world has influenced how we view and approach dating relationships, often in many ways we don't even recognize.

However, positive change is ahead, as we present the following:

- An approach to dating that is both intentional, yet fun

- Ten fresh perspectives on dating that are both inspiring, yet realistic

- Six prerequisites to prepare you for the adventure of dating

- Ten different subjects you'll want to address before moving a dating relationship to the engagement phase

- The one thing everyone should know about marriage before they ever date

This chapter marks the end of the fourth lesson in an 8-week LoveEd study. For discussion questions and resources go to:

FMUniversity.net/DatePrep-wk4

CHAPTER 11:
A FRIENDS-FIRST APPROACH TO DATING

The content of the previous half of this book came out of a live discussion series I originally presented on Christian college campuses called *Friends Don't Let Friends Date Dumb.* I only wished to point out the dangers of dating while ignoring God's word, science, and logic.

But after my presentations, students would come up wondering what they *should* be doing. They weren't content just to know what to *avoid.* They wanted to know what to *seek.*

For the longest time I wasn't willing to go down that road, because I feared falling into the pit of Joshua Harris, author of *I Kissed Dating Goodbye,* where people would treat my book like a bible and then blame me when everything didn't work out for them like they hoped.

However, I felt compelled to address the need, and so with fear and trepidation, over many years and with much prayer, I drafted and refined a different approach to dating that we will introduce to you in this chapter.

But before we get to that, allow me to share some core truths about seeking God's will in any part of your life.

"SO YOU WANT MY OPINION NOW?"

You may remember I went out with many lovely lovers of the Lord my freshman year of college. You would probably not be surprised to learn that I wished to do more of the same my sophomore year.

But that was before I met Danielle (not her real name).

Suddenly, I didn't want to date around anymore. I wanted to date Danielle. And only Danielle. She was drop-dead gorgeous with a razor-sharp wit and a heart for God. I fell hard for her. Really hard.

The trick was that Danielle didn't feel the same way. As shocking as that may be to you.

So, I set out to win her heart with the most intricate dating adventure I ever endeavored to pull off: the "Total Recall" date, inspired by the sci-fi flick starring Arnold Schwarzenegger. Don't watch the movie, but just know in *Total Recall* you can never decide if Arnold Schwarzenegger is the good guy on the run from the bad guys or the bad guy on the run from the good guys.

In any case, my plan involved a cast of several friends posing as government agents and nefarious criminals. After accepting my date invitation, the week leading up to our date, Danielle started receiving TOP SECRET packages and had to carry out clandestine missions that would cause her to question "who I really was." One minute it would seem like I was a government agent, the next, a foreign spy.

On the day of our big date, we were to wind up at the intramural fields in the late afternoon where we would suddenly be pinned down in the middle of an epic (cap) gun battle until—just in the nick of time—we'd be whisked away in a black sedan for our evening together. (Keep in mind, this was before people were actually shooting people on school campuses, so I anticipated this little skirmish causing a buzz on campus, but not a 911 call.)

We'll never know how that grand finale would have gone. Danielle got cold feet and backed out of the week-long, role-playing part of our date. I guess you could say the Total Recall date wound up being *recalled*.

I was embarrassed. I mean, I scared this girl away. Not with the fake guns, but with my very real interest in her.

And I was mad at God because I felt like I had done all the right things and didn't deserve to have my heart broken. How did I fall so hard for a girl who was never going to fall for me? "Why would God let that happen?" I wondered.

I will never forget God's lightning-quick reply, "Oh, so you want my opinion *now*?"

Want His opinion now?! What was that supposed to mean? Hadn't I been doing the dating thing right? Hadn't I determined only to ask out girls who love Jesus? Hadn't I kept my dating life pure?

I was incensed by His answer, and I let Him know it.

And He let me have my little tantrum. I reviewed my spotless relational résumé with God and awaited His understanding response.

But I don't remember getting any. Instead, I remember finally asking Him, "So did you want me to ask *You* about Danielle specifically *before* I asked her out?"

I knew the answer even as I asked the question.

Of course! The God of the Bible doesn't want us to just follow a bunch of rules. He wants us to follow *Him*. Was it really any different with Adam and Eve, or Noah, or Abraham, or Moses, or the nation of Israel?

DO YOU WANT TO FOLLOW PRINCIPLES OR A PERSON?

Do you know how many times God is referred to as "the LORD your God" or "the LORD our God" or "the LORD my God"? It's 402, 100, and 39 times respectively. That's almost 550 times total.

That word, "LORD" (in all caps), is the name God revealed to Moses through the burning bush. It bears huge weight in meaning: the self-existent One, the One who is that He is, the God who can't be simplified down to a simple definition.

Unlike the gods of other religions, who were the god of the sea, or the wind, or the mountains, the God of the Bible is the God of all that is. Nothing exists apart from His infinite sovereignty.

> Oh, the depth of the riches and wisdom and knowledge of God!
> How unsearchable are his judgments and how inscrutable his
> ways! "For who has known the mind of the Lord, or who has been
> his counselor? Or who has given a gift to him that he might be
> repaid?" For from him and through him and to him are all things.
> To him be glory forever. Amen. —Romans 11:33-36 ESV

But despite His vast magnificence, He exists *not* apart and aloof from His creation, but in close relationship.

> The Lord is near to all who call on him, to all who call on him in
> truth. He fulfills the desire of those who fear him; he also hears
> their cry and saves them. The Lord preserves all who love him,
> but all the wicked he will destroy. My mouth will speak the praise
> of the Lord, and let all flesh bless his holy name forever and ever.
> —Psalm 145:18-21 ESV

He is indeed the LORD, but he's also mine and wants to be yours, that He might be ours. So He's not only the Self-existent One, but the Self-existent One who belongs to us. He's not only the One who is that He is, but the

One who is that He is for the good of you and me. And the LORD our God wants us to follow *Him*. Personally.

So, as you read the suggestions to come for dating in God's will, know I'm less interested in compelling you to follow a set of principles as I am in inviting you to follow a person, the LORD our God.

You can follow the principles, yet lose sight of the Person, just like I did. But if you follow the Person, then His principles will guard and guide you in all of life.

A GREAT GRADE IS *NOT* THE GOAL

On the topic of following a person instead of just principles, I have a confession to make. I am a recovering legalist. I certainly don't want to encourage you to be one. I don't even want to encourage you to be a law-keeper, really. I'd rather encourage you to be a law-*lover*.

Both the law-keeper and the law-lover will endeavor to keep the law, but only one for the right motive.

Let me illustrate with a quick story from early in my marriage.

I was out jogging one day when I saw a girl up ahead with a perfect body in a jog bra, and my mind started to wander (if you know what I mean). After she was out of sight, I was still fighting lustful thoughts.

Part of my struggle involved prayer, and so at one point I said, "God, if I was ever about to cheat on Julie, I wish you would have a car come out of nowhere, like right now while I'm crossing the street, and kill me before I ever get the chance to dishonor you in that way."

God's response was as clear as if I had heard His voice out loud.

"You know, you are really more interested in getting an 'A' than you are in learning the material."

God nailed it. (Of course He did.) That's exactly the way I thought. I wanted to keep the law, and I wanted an "A." If I was about to fail a test, I'd rather just die instead. What's wrong with that?

Why would God want another failed disciple? Why wouldn't He want a bunch of straight-A students representing Him in the world?

Can you relate to me? Then you could be tempted to read this book (or the Bible, or any other discipleship book) with the desire of getting an "A."

- A flawless dating life free not only of sin, but free of rejection, heartbreak, and regret.

- A flawless engagement free not only of sin, but free of stress, miscommunication, and conflict.

- A flawless marriage free not only of sin, but free of disappointment, discouragement, and disagreements.

All the while, God wants to use rejection, stress, disappointment—all of it—to help you "learn the material." He uses such things (everything, really) to empower us to learn the lessons He knows we need to learn, in order to become the kind of people He created us to be.

He's not interested in followers with spotless records. He's interested in followers with spotless hearts, hearts tested and tried through temptations and trials, even if that entails occasionally succumbing to both.

The person who just wants to keep the law will only care about their grade, while the person who *loves* the law will want to learn the material. Which are you naturally? Which would you like to be?

HOW FUN IS HOOKING UP, REALLY?

Not everyone is a legalist. Some don't care about their grade. Instead, they want to pass, while getting away with as much as they can.

Maybe that's you. You want to do enough to keep God happy, while doing enough to keep yourself happy.

Does your fear of missing out (FOMO) have you looking to take advantage of every possible loophole in God's law?

I can relate to this perspective too. Even though I preferred judging the heathens in my life over joining them, I still assumed they were having more fun than I was. I just believed delayed gratification would pay off in the end.

However, as it turns out, when it comes to the "sexual freedom" indulged in on a regular basis by students immersed in the hookup culture, immediate gratification isn't all that gratifying.

In fact, research conducted by Dr. Donna Freitas reveals that the majority of students hooking up on college campuses today don't actually feel all that great about it, using words like "dirty," "used," "empty," and "regretful" to describe their last sexual experience.[5]

Granted that only includes a slight majority of males, so almost half of the guys are having the theoretical time of their lives, but prior to reading Dr. Freitas's research, I would have assumed almost 100% of at least the male college students would have nothing but praise for hooking up.

At the end of the day, you need to decide who you're going to trust:

- Cultural propaganda or the Creator's word
- Fleeting passions or faithful principles
- Your limited experience or the experience of adults who have "been there done that" (or perhaps the experience of college students in an unbiased research study)

---

[5] Donna Freitas, *The End of Sex: How Hookup Culture Is Leaving a Generation Unhappy, Sexually Unfulfilled, and Confused about Intimacy,* Google Books (Basic Books, April 2, 2013), https://books.google.com/books?id=aKKECVcNWskC&dq=donna%2Bfreitas %2B%E2%80%9CDashed%2Bhopes%E2%80%9D.

WHAT IS FRIENDS-FIRST DATING?

With those caveats, allow me to now introduce a fresh approach to dating.

> **Friends-First Dating:** Intentional time invested in one other
> person for the purpose of growing a friendship that might
> lead to a life-giving, lifelong marriage

You may love that definition right away or you may not, but know this. Our definition is the fruit of about ten years of prayer, Bible study, research, and wise counsel, so though it's certainly not perfect, consider giving it the benefit of the doubt.

Perhaps considering the perspective we present could be the key to formulating your *own* approach.

DATE ON PURPOSE. NOT BY ACCIDENT.

The first word of our definition is "intentional," which means friends-first dating does not include any of the following relational practices:

- Hanging out—Hanging out with the purpose of growing in friendship is great! It's even a fantastic precursor to dating, but it's *not* dating.

- Unplanned meetings—Frequent meetings which occur out of happenstance or habit (at the gym, over lunch, after work, or in church) are another great way to get to know someone before dating, but again it's *not* dating.

- Texting—Texting can be a very intimate form of communication, but by its nature it is not intentional. You text when you have a chance. They text back when they have the chance. And so on. This is *not* dating.

In contrast, friends-first dating is dating done with purpose. Not by accident. By definition, intentionality is part of the deal.

That doesn't mean friends-first dating can't be relaxed, fun, silly, and imaginative. In fact, we think it should be all those things. But what it shouldn't be is aimless.

WHAT INVESTING IN "ONE OTHER PERSON" *DOESN'T* MEAN

We believe dating should be uniquely different from other social engagements, not only in its intentionality, but also in its focus on one other person.

However, let me clarify what we *don't* mean by that.

For starters, as we've already established, you should always involve your community in your dating life, so "intentional time invested in one other person" should never involve ditching your friends (remember dating don't #1) nor isolating when you're on a date (remember dating don't #4).

"Intentional time invested in one other person" also doesn't rule out group dating. Indeed, we love the idea of group dating. A lot. Everyone is still coupled up, but each individual can enjoy the company of the group as much as they enjoy the company of their own date.

Double, triple, and quadruple dates can be far more comfortable and fun, giving everyone the freedom to "just be themselves." This can eliminate the pressure and awkwardness common in the early stages of one-on-one dates—especially first dates.

Further, as long as the couples involved don't treat the date like a PDA (public display of affection) competition, the social dynamics of group dating can curb preoccupation with romance and sexual tension. Less focus on romantic and physical intimacy enables you to focus more on emotional and relational intimacy, both within the group and between each couple.

Lastly, "intentional time invested in one other person" doesn't mean only dating one person at a time.

Of course, we're not advising you to go out with a different person every weekend (like I almost managed to do my freshman year in college). That's not particularly healthy. We're definitely not suggesting you carry on a serious dating relationship with more than one person at a time. We don't want to promote love triangles or rectangles or any other love shapes. Except hearts.

However, if you keep your dates platonic and focused on growing friendships, even as you gauge the possibility of mutual attraction, "dating around" is fine. You're still investing time in one other person on each date, and you're not taking advantage of anyone.

However, as soon as things clearly start moving beyond friendship (i.e., you're holding hands, kissing, or even staring into each other's eyes in ways that would be weird for you to do with a sibling), you both need to be open and honest about that. If the attraction seems to be mutual, then you need to discuss the wisdom of making your dating relationship exclusive.

So that's what we mean by "intentional time invested in one other person." Or at least what we *don't* mean.

HOW WOULD JESUS DATE?

Let's use Jesus as our example. Though He never dated, He was definitely intentional about relationships. He called out each of His twelve disciples and then invested in them, especially Peter, James, and John.

Much of His teaching focused on how to live in healthy relationships, especially His sermon on the mount (recorded in Matthew, chapters 5-7) and His final words to His disciples (as recorded in John, chapters 13-17).

Jesus was so intentional about relationships that, even as He hung on the cross, writhing in pain as He slowly suffocated to death, three of His final seven statements were about the needs of those He cared about. That included His mother (whom He ensured would be taken care of by one of His disciples), one of the thieves on the cross (whom He personally forgave), and His enemies mocking Him (whom He asked God to forgive).

Don't you think Jesus would have been just as intentional about dating, had that been part of the plan? More pointedly, don't you think he'd want *us* to be that intentional?

So instead of trying to *impress* your date, look to *invest* in them! Even in the midst of a notorious first date fail, you can pray like Jesus, "Father, forgive them, for they know not what they do."

CHAPTER 12:

10 FRESH PERSPECTIVES ON DATING TO CHANGE YOUR RELATIONSHIP LIFE

Proverbs 29:18 warns us, "Without a vision the people perish."

The Hebrew word for "perish" is also interpreted as "cast off restraint" or "run wild." So put that all together and the passage is basically saying, "Without a vision, people cast off restraint and run wild. Until they die."

Doesn't that sound a bit like contemporary dating? Middle schoolers date without ever going on dates, high school and college students hook up without ever going on dates, and young adults into their 30s date online without ever going on dates and without getting any closer to marriage than they were back in middle school.

Since that isn't the kind of dating future you want, this chapter and the two that follow are designed to empower you to cast a vision for dating that's both realistic *and* inspiring, by sharing ten fresh perspectives on dating to change your relationship life.

PERSPECTIVE #1: DATE BECAUSE YOU'RE CALLED

What about dating, not just because you *can*, but because you're *called*? You know, like dating had a goal you wanted—and even felt led to achieve.

If that were so, what do you think you should be called to before you date?

A. Pulling the movie move
B. A significant other
C. Making out
D. Marriage

It's not supposed to be a trick question. It's actually our first vision for dating. Date because you know you are called to *marriage*.

I'm not saying you should only date someone you think you're *supposed* to marry. That's more like arranged marriage than dating.

Instead, we present friends-first dating as the process by which you seek to discern who you're supposed to marry. Indeed, this is how dating has been traditionally viewed since its inception in our modern culture. Naturally, this would assume you can't know if you're supposed to marry someone until you've dated them. And not just once or twice, but for some time.

Sure, no one wants to date only to break up, but if you're dating wisely, breaking up doesn't have to be devastating, and since you can't predict the future, some level of risk is necessary.

However, if you're not sure you're called to marriage in the first place, then don't date. Dating is for those who believe they are called to marriage.

How to Know If You're Called to Marriage

Are you called to marriage? Ironically, this question is best answered by a biblical author who made it clear he was *not* called to marriage.

In 1 Corinthians 7:7, the Apostle Paul expressed the desire for all to live a life of celibate singleness like himself. In spite of his hopes, he knew most would not be able to join him on his crusade of sexlessness. Instead, in verses 8 and 9, he states the following:

> *To the unmarried and the widows I say that it is good for them to remain single, as I am. But if they cannot exercise self-control, they should marry. For it is better to marry than to burn with passion.*
> —1 Corinthians 7:8-9 ESV

So how does this passage identify who is called to celibacy and who is called to marriage? Put simply, Paul suggests your sex drive will tell you.

- Is sexual temptation not really a problem for you?
  You ought to seriously consider whether you
  might be called to celibacy.

- Is exercising self-control a continual struggle?
  You can safely assume you're called to marriage.

Marriage Isn't About Sex

Of course, Paul isn't promoting marriage as the solution to your lust problem. Everyone must eventually learn to exercise self-control in all areas of temptation, including sexual temptation. *Especially* sexual temptation.

This reality is why marriage is the best reason to wait for sex, but sex is the worst reason to rush into marriage. Because marriage isn't about sex. It's the other way around.

Sex is about marriage, and marriage is about relationship: first your relationship with your spouse and then your relationship with any children your marriage may bring to life. And all the while, God designed the marriage relationship to illustrate the supernatural relationships of both God the Father with His Son, and His Son with His church.

So we see that marriage wasn't created to bless sex. Sex was created to bless marriage, as it represents and facilitates the oneness of marriage.

You Are Probably Called to Marriage

To be clear, you don't have to possess a sex drive that's off the chain, stuck in overdrive, and high on crack to know you're called to marriage. You could simply long for that oneness: the companionship, the connection, the relational intimacy of marriage.

Could you be wrong? Could you think your sex drive or your marital longings are telling you you're supposed to be married, when, for whatever reason, God intends for you to embrace a life of celibacy?

It is possible, but based on Paul's words, I don't think God could blame you for guessing wrong. Paul certainly wouldn't, as he stated flatly earlier in his letter:

> But because of the temptation to sexual immorality, each man
> should have his own wife and each woman her own husband.
> —1 Corinthians 7:2 ESV

What About Love at First Sight?

While I'm saying you shouldn't have to know if you'll marry someone before you date them, the reality is many believe they *do* know who they're supposed to marry before they date. Some even believe in love at first sight!

More significantly, many Christian couples believe God told them who they would marry before they ever dated. Sort of like God's call to marriage at first sight!

However, here is the indisputable reality among Christians who believe God told them who they would marry before they ever dated (or even met) their partner:

- Some are happily married today.
  (Does this prove "thus saith the Lord?")

- Some are miserable in their marriage today.
  (Is *that* what God wanted?)

- Some are divorced today.
  (Did God tell them to get divorced too?)

- Some never married.
  (Because the dating relationship didn't work out.)

- Some never even dated.
  (Because God never told the other person.)

I even know some people personally who have had several different individuals claim to be God's marital choice for them. (Does God bless polygamy now?)

My point is this: while the kind of love that can sustain a lifelong, sacrificial relationship like marriage may be intense and driven by devotion, it's never rash and never driven by hormones and impulses. (Remember 1 Corinthians 13: Love is *patient!*)

That said, I believe God may well tell some who they will marry before they date. And maybe He'll do that with you.

However, even if you believe God has revealed His marital will for you early on in a relationship (or before), He will *not* be the least bit offended if you want to take the time to get to know the person before you get engaged. Further, taking the time to seek clarity through His word, as well as the counsel and prayers of those you look up to in the faith, could not possibly upset Him.

This behavior does not demonstrate a lack of faith. It demonstrates wisdom! (That's one of God's preferred love languages.)

Beware of Following Your Heart

God is well aware that we are spiritually undiscerning most of the time.

> *As it is written: "None is righteous, no, not one; no one*
> *understands; no one seeks for God. All have turned aside;*
> *together they have become worthless; no one does good,*
> *not even one."* —Romans 3:10-12 ESV

He knows we're particularly compromised when it comes to the longings of our heart.

> *The heart is deceitful above all things, and desperately sick; ...*
> —Jeremiah 17:9a ESV

Indeed, many a strong and true believer has been deceived by their own heart.

Instead of *knowing* the will of God in romance, they were actually only *feeling* their own will. This is why, after warning us that "the heart is deceitful above all things, and desperately sick," The Prophet Jeremiah finishes verse 9 by asking:

> *... who can understand it?* —Jeremiah 17:9b ESV

Thankfully, God answers Jerry's question in the following verse:

> *"I the Lord search the heart and test the mind, to give every man*
> *according to his ways, according to the fruit of his deeds."*
> —Jeremiah 17:10 ESV

So, if you believe God has revealed "the one" to you before you've thoroughly gotten to know "the one," why not give yourself several months to search your own heart and test your own mind. Better yet, seek *His* heart and understanding.

What God Told Me about My Wife before We Dated

I totally understand that desire to want to know if you're going to marry someone before you ever date them. It certainly takes away all the guess-work, right?

I'll never forget a conversation I had with God before Julie and I started dating. I share the dialogue below, but know these words are not in the Bible, and I didn't transcribe the conversation, so God's words are merely paraphrased.

God: You know if you and Julie wanted to date more seriously, I would like that.

Me: You would like that because she's "the one"?

God: I'm just saying that if you and Julie wanted to take your relationship to the next level that would please me.

Me: That would please you because you want us to get married?

God didn't answer. God did not tell me I was to marry Julie. God didn't even tell me to date her, but through that prayer conversation, I clearly sensed God's blessing on asking Julie if she wanted to enter a serious dating relationship.

I also had the blessing of my pastor and two accountability partners whom I met with weekly, along with my best friend and my mom, all who knew me inside and out and wanted God's best for my life. So I wasn't just moving forward based on voices I was hearing in my head.

Still, asking Julie to be my girlfriend was a huge step of faith, one I believed God was happy for me to take. But I truly had no idea where that would lead us.

For we walk by faith, not by sight. —2 Corinthians 5:7 ESV

You Can't Follow God's Will in the Future

Many times we believe God's will is about the future, about where He's taking us, or more honestly about where we *want* Him to take us, but God's will is always—always—about where He's leading us right now.

God never asks us to follow Him in the future. He asks us to follow Him in the present. Even in your dating life. *Especially* in your dating life.

Take this moment, for instance. I believe you are walking in God's will right now as you're reading these words, even as I am walking in God's will right now as I type them, praying this book would be daily bread for you on your journey through dating to marriage.

Stop Seeking God's Will

Spoiler alert: if you determine to seek God's will, you may still miss it.

No, that wasn't a typo. If you truly, earnestly seek God's will you can still miss it.

Because, ultimately, it isn't God's will to give you His will. Ultimately, God wants to give us something far greater than His will.

He wants to give us Himself!

This means God's will, whether it be in your dating life or any other life pursuit, is less about *doing* and more about *being*. Less about doing His work and more about being with Him.

So stop worrying about God's will for your future marriage and simply walk with Him in this study as you prepare to date with purpose. Then walk with Him in every relationship that may lead to dating and then in each dating relationship. If you endeavor to follow Him one day at a time, when you will look back, you won't see what *you* did, but what *He* did. And how He led you every step of the way.

If you truly believe God wants to and *will* guide you in dating, then you can date like you're called to marriage, without being obsessed with marriage.

PERSPECTIVE #2: DATE LIKE NO ONE'S DOING IT

In the Top 10 Dumbest Reasons to Date, we talked about the temptation to date because everyone's doing it, but what about dating like *no one's* doing it?

In other words, date like you are set apart from the world for the glory of God!

> *But you are a chosen race, a royal priesthood, a holy nation, a people for his own possession, that you may proclaim the excellencies of him who called you out of darkness into his marvelous light. Once you were not a people, but now you are God's people; once you had not received mercy, but now you have received mercy. Beloved, I urge you as sojourners and exiles to abstain from the passions of the flesh, which wage war against your soul. Keep your conduct among the Gentiles honorable, so that when they speak against you as evildoers, they may see your good deeds and glorify God on the day of visitation.* —1 Peter 2:9-12 ESV

Let that vision inspire you to date like no one's doing it. Not just to stand out, but to stand out for our God! Consider these principles:

- Live for God's glory over your desired love story.
- Trust God's goodness over the world's rewards.
- Follow timeless wisdom over pop culture advice.
- Prioritize your future purpose over passing pleasures.
- Treat your date as better than yourself.

So often we want to live for God in some areas but live for ourselves in other areas. In no other area of life is that temptation greater than in dating, and in no other are the stakes higher.

Your dating decisions are critical! They will determine who you marry, when you marry, or whether you marry at all.

Foolish dating decisions have to be overcome by wiser decisions after marriage, whereas wise dating decisions intentionally establish your future marriage on a firm foundation.

Trust me, if your marriage is built on a firm foundation, you will go from dating like no one else to being married like no one else. (Especially in a time when so few are marrying at all.)

PERSPECTIVE #3: DATE TO MAKE FRIENDS

Here's the love story the media has tried to sell you: you need to find "that special someone" who's as crazy about you as you are about them and then you marry and live happily ever after.

Have you bought into this narrative?

If so, you should know that research reveals the intense feelings of being madly in love are temporary. Always. No exceptions.

Those emotions are the result of brain chemistry—a condition psychologists call limerence. And the neurochemistry of limerence generally lasts only six months to two years.[6] Tops. (More about the chemistry of limerence in Chapter 15.)

Now maybe you know (or have heard about) an elderly couple who disputes this scientific conclusion. I'm talking about couples who claim to be more in love today than they were when they married 30, 40, 50+ years ago.

---

[6] Joe Beam, *"I'm in Love with Another; What Should I Do?,"* Crosswalk.com (Crosswalk.com, December 12, 2011), https://www.crosswalk.com/family/marriage/i-m-in-love-with-another-man.html.

The ironic thing is, I would say the same thing about my own marriage which is almost 30 years old. Our love is far more rich and meaningful than it was in our dating and courtship.

But it's not the same kind of love. In other words, we are not continually thinking about each other. Our hearts don't race when we see one another. We don't tremble when we hold hands. And we don't want to jump in the sack and get frisky every single night. And day.

All of that may sound sad to you, and I hate to disappoint. Yet, please believe me. This love is far from disappointing. It's steady, true, and empowering. It's a connection I couldn't have conceived of when Julie and I married.

I guess the reality is you can't know how it would feel to invest decades pouring your life out for someone, as they pour their life out for you, until you've done it with someone.

In contrast, almost everyone knows what it feels like to fall in love. Many know what it feels like to fall in love with someone who falls in love with them too. But few know what my wife and I have done from experience.

Our love today is so much deeper and broader and greater than the feelings we shared as young lovers. It's why we do what we do at FMU. Because we want you to enjoy a marriage like ours.

However, if the love Julie and I share today doesn't so much exude the romantic magic of chick lit, how would I best describe our union?

Friendship. A deep, abiding friendship.

Yes, a friendship with benefits. In fact, we're *best* friends with benefits, but after all the sacrifices and blessings of a faithful marriage, those benefits extend far beyond the sexual. Indeed, saying Julie and I are "best friends" doesn't quite capture how we feel about each other, since most best friends haven't lived together for 28 years, investing 26+ of those years in raising kids together.

This is why our third vision for dating encourages you to date to make friends.

The Purpose of Dating Is Not Marriage

To clarify, if you want to go out with someone, you ought to be open to the idea of becoming more than friends. Otherwise, why date them? After all, the goal of friends-first dating is a life-giving, lifelong marriage.

But while marriage is the *goal* of friends-first dating, it's not the *purpose*. The *goal* of friends-first dating is marriage, but the *purpose* is growing a friendship.

What If You Grow In Love Instead of Fall?

If you can only allow yourself to be attracted to the hottest person in the room, that says something about you. And it isn't good.

And I was guilty! In fact, this approach to dating almost had me leave college single instead of engaged to the woman I've been telling you so much about in this book. How tragic had I missed my chance to win the heart of a super woman because I was set on winning the heart of a supermodel?

We're not saying ignore your feelings! Feelings may not be facts, but they are information. However, don't let chemistry dictate your dating decisions.

Neither Julie nor I were interested in dating seriously when we first met, nor after our first date, nor after getting to know each other as friends. But after two and a half years, our friendship grew so much that a romantic attraction caught fire. Even though we talked about eventually falling in love (and it did indeed feel that way), the reality is that we more or less *grew* in love.

What Julie and I did by accident, we're suggesting you pursue on purpose.

Date to Make Friends, Not *Pretend* to Make Friends

There is a difference between dating to make friends and *pretending* to make friends. I am talking about the bait-and-switch dater. Bait-and-switch dating is when you identify your crush (and by that I mean the person you can't stop thinking about and can hardly talk to without slurred speech), and you ask them out "as just friends."

You may take this approach because you suspect (or know) they don't feel anything else other than friendship for you. Or you may take this approach simply because you lack the courage to be honest. Either way, you bait them into dating you by declaring your undying desire for "just" friendship.

All the while, you're waiting for that right opportunity when you'll pull the switch and reveal all your deepest feelings for them, hoping they feel the same way! So essentially, you're deceiving them. You begin the relationship on pretense, and that's never a good way to begin. Unless you're a spy.

Depressurize Your Dating Life

Do you know the beauty of making friendship instead of marriage the purpose of your dating life? It takes so much pressure off of you!

If marriage is not only the goal, but also the whole purpose of your dating life, then you can't be successful until you wind up married.

- Every first date that doesn't lead to a second is a failure.
- Every second date that doesn't lead to a third date is a failure.
- Every dating relationship that doesn't end in marriage is a failure.

Is that how you want to date: pass or fail?

But if friendship is your purpose, then every date can be a success. This is true even if a date doesn't go well. Because learning you're not able to click with someone as friends tells you all you need to know to move on from that relationship without any hearts having to break.

When the purpose of dating is friendship, then the persistent question isn't, "Are we going to get married?" The persistent question is, "Are we growing a great friendship?" The question you're trying to answer doesn't require predicting the future of your relationship but gauging the present state of it.

If, as you're dating to make friends, one of you develops feelings while the other not so much, that's obviously disappointing, but then you can still part as friends, allowing you both to heal and look elsewhere for that friendship where the feelings will be mutually reciprocated.

However, if the two of you keep growing in mutual encouragement, enjoyment, understanding, respect, and trust, keep going out. Then, if a romance blossoms out of a friendship you've spent a year or more growing, you can more confidently look at the possibility of marriage in the future.

CHAPTER 13:

CASTING A VISION FOR YOUR DATING LIFE

To set up our next fresh perspective on dating, allow me to share a tale of two bachelors.

Bachelor #1: Meet Mark. Ever since Mark started watching the Disney channel in third grade, the goal of his dating life was … well … more or less simply having a dating life.

So, when he found out in middle school that Taylor had a crush on him, he asked her to the school dance. From that point on, this was his pattern for dating: whenever he learned an attractive girl found *him* attractive, he asked her out.

The beauty of this approach? Mark was never disappointed when he asked a girl out. They not only would agree to a date, they would invariably agree to a steady dating relationship. Oftentimes even before an actual date.

But Mark never seemed satisfied in his dating relationships, and neither did his girlfriends. So when the initial excitement of falling in love subsided, Mark was already on the hunt for a new love interest.

That said, at least he was meeting the goal of his dating life: to have a dating life! However, it was an empty one with little to show for it but memories and regrets. By his senior year in college, Mark pretty much gave up on dating. He figured hooking up allowed him to get to the best part of dating right away, without any expectations to meet beyond that.

Bachelor #2: Meet John. John believed the goal of his dating life ought to be marriage, so it didn't make sense to ask a girl out just because he knew she'd say "yes."

That included Bailey, who crushed on him in middle school. After all, what's the odds of marrying your middle school sweetheart, right? Especially if her family is going to move to Kokomo the summer before high school. Which they did.

It also meant not dating Tiffany, the varsity cheerleader who liked him but didn't like church. John wanted a wife who loved God as much as he did.

Speaking of God, there was one girl from youth group with whom John shared a mutual attraction. Megan not only loved God, she lived for Him. She even felt called to foreign missions. This was definitely the sort of girl John could imagine marrying, but since he didn't feel called to foreign missions himself, they determined to enjoy a friendship. They even went to prom as friends but then left for their separate colleges with no regrets.

After dating several sweet, Christian girls in college, John entered his first serious relationship his sophomore year. Sadly, things with Sarah didn't work out, but they didn't view that as a failure. He was dating to get married, not to marry everyone he dated, and they had dated long enough to see they weren't right for each other.

Then something surprising happened in John's senior year: he felt a call to foreign missions. In fact, he wound up going to a missions' conference before graduating, and guess who he ran into there?

Megan was even more surprised to see John, but they had a blast reconnecting. John didn't know how things would turn out, but now dating

Megan made a lot more sense. Especially when they realized they shared a heart for China.

PERSPECTIVE #4: DATE FOR THE ADVENTURE

Obviously dating with the goal of marriage made all the difference between our two bachelors, but why?

Without a goal for his dating life beyond simply having a dating life, Mark had no criteria or purpose to guide his dating pursuits, so he basically took advantage of whatever opportunities came his way.

In contrast to a series of disconnected opportunities in the moment, John treated dating like an epic adventure with marriage as its destination. His goal not only guided his dating pursuits but lent meaning and significance to every date, even the long-term relationship that didn't work out.

So instead of taking advantage of any and every opportunity that comes your way, date like you want your dating life to take you somewhere. Date for the adventure!

Dating: Opportunity or Adventure? Pick One!

An adventure differs vastly from an opportunity in four key ways:

- An adventure has a greater goal.
- An adventure has a higher purpose.
- An adventure has a longer time horizon.
- An adventure requires more preparation.

When you set out to simply take advantage of whatever opportunities "love" throws your way, then your dating life just happens to you. Or it doesn't.

Can you see how this gives you a sense of control whenever you take advantage of each opportunity, even as it renders you powerless to influence the long-term direction of your dating life?

In contrast, treating your dating life like an adventure, with the goal of a life-giving, lifelong marriage, can inspire you to prepare and persevere with a sense of purpose. Even through tough times.

Then that very perseverance which enables you to reach the altar and make your vows becomes the perfect preparation for the adventure of marriage, when you must *fulfill* your vows, day after day. This is where perseverance will take on a whole new meaning and significance. Especially if you end up raising children together.

An Adventure Is about the Journey as Much as It Is about the Goal

For an adventure to be successful, you want to achieve your goal. However, the end can never justify the means, because a noble goal cannot be reached in ignoble ways. So along the journey of a great adventure, every mile matters.

Further, the very significance of the goal you are trying to reach on an adventure imbues your journey with great import. You have that higher purpose. You know you're in it for the long haul. You even prepare in earnest before you ever launch out: praying, maturing, studying, training, and assembling your crew.

Likewise, in the adventure of dating, determine you will do all in your power to reach your goal and then move forward with purpose. If all you can do is prepare as you wait on the Lord, then do so. No prayer will go unheard. No step in maturity will prove meaningless. No truth will return void. No discipline will be for not. No wise counsel will fail you.

Please be encouraged, my friend, even if your dating life has drifted off course, or you're struggling to keep your ship afloat on tempestuous seas, or if you quite literally haven't seen a breeze in years. Or your entire life.

You're on an adventure. Did you expect it to be easy?

Nay, me laddie. But worth the journey? You bet your boots!

The True End of Your Adventure Is Not Marriage

Whether it includes marriage or not, God is calling you on an adventure. And the most amazing part is that He doesn't wish to merely send you. He wants to go *with* you every mile of your journey!

If your dating journey doesn't end in marriage, you will not miss it in the end. By the end, I mean when you see Him face-to-face and hear Him say, "Well done, my good and faithful servant!"

Even if you do get married, when you appear before the throne, you'll see so clearly that marriage was never the ultimate goal. The ultimate goal was to conform you into Christ's image, and marriage was one of the main refining tools to get you there.

PERSPECTIVE #5: DATE AND CHANGE THE WORLD

What ideas come to mind when you think of changing the world?

Do you imagine saving souls, saving the environment, or both? Perhaps you think of inventing a new technology, writing a book, discovering the cure to cancer, or starting a band which will be more than a band. It will become a movement. Perhaps your music will "help put an end to war and poverty. It will align the planets and bring them into universal harmony, allowing meaningful contact with all forms of life, from extraterrestrial beings to common household pets." (Perhaps I was just quoting Rufus from *Bill and Ted's Excellent Adventure*. "Yes, way!")

Whatever you come up with, my guess is you probably wouldn't think of dating as a means of changing the world, and you probably didn't think of marriage either.

However, I would like to suggest that if leaving the world a better place is high on your priority list, then getting married and starting a family is more likely to get you there than digging wells in developing nations, reversing global warming, fighting for your country, or feeding the hungry.

If You Want to Change the World, You've Got to Get Personal

According to our culture today, the pathway to world change requires becoming an influencer, more than likely a social media influencer.

I totally get that perspective. I mean, I didn't write over 410 posts and shoot over 260 videos with no desire to influence anyone online. Guilty!

Even this book was written in the hopes of not only changing the course of your dating life, but your *entire* life. So, I'm guilty again.

However, regardless of who reads this book, when my time on earth is done, the greatest impact I will leave behind, for better or for worse, will be felt and recognized by those who knew me personally: first and foremost, my wife and children. And I can tell you, beyond a shadow of a doubt, that the human being who has made the single greatest difference in my own life (after Christ) is my wife, Julie. And before I met her, it was my parents.

Perhaps you'll leave a mark on the world bigger than Einstein or Mother Teresa. But even their biggest impact was known by those who knew them best and loved them most. Up close! Not from afar. The same will be true of you.

It was even true of Jesus. Think about it. Jesus never sought to build a platform. He simply endeavored to pour His life into His disciples, inspiring them to, in turn, pour their lives out for those who knew them personally.

Even today, Jesus can powerfully influence, bless, and direct our lives because we can know Him personally. Up close! Not from afar.

How Can a Marriage Change the World?

Instead of seeking to build a platform to change the world, what if you sought out a life partner with a similar passion for world change?

> *Two are better than one, because they have a good reward*
> *for their toil.* —Ecclesiastes 4:9 ESV

Can you make a difference on your own? Of course! Do you have to get married to make a difference with someone else? Of course not! That's what the church is all about: making a difference together for Christ.

But that's also what the family is all about! Indeed, a church can only be as healthy as the families which make it up.

In fact, marriage has been the foundation of every stable society across time and culture. And there's a reason for that. From the beginning, when God saw that Adam was alone, he designed marriage to meet our deep need for relational intimacy, and in doing so, to create the optimum environment to raise up future generations to marry and do the same.

As a result, when a man and a woman bear children but aren't committed to one another—don't even stay together—the stats reveal those children are far more likely to experience a plethora of negative outcomes.

So the world changes. But not for the better.

However, when a couple not only marries, but faithfully covenants to love, honor, and cherish one another until death and then proceeds to do just that, year after year, decade after decade, the world changes for the better. Even if that couple never has children of their own.

That's how a marriage can change the world.

And if the purpose of marriage is less about living happily ever after and more about living to make the world a better place, how should that affect the way you date?

Change the World One Date at a Time

Consider this: everyone is changed by a serious dating relationship.

You can't help but be changed by someone you let into your heart, but what kind of change is that for most people? Good? Not usually, because so many are out there dating to get their needs met or secure the life they want.

But what if we dated to change the world? For good!

Why not begin by carrying yourself with such honor and grace that everyone you date is better for having known you, and everyone you enter into a serious relationship with is truly blessed by the experience?

Gentlemen, what if your conduct toward every woman you date leads her to know she is worthy of love, honor, and care, even if the date doesn't go well?

Ladies, what if your behavior toward every man you date leads him to know he is worthy of kindness, respect, and appreciation, even if he doesn't turn out to be your type?

Further, if you date to change the world, you won't just impact those you date, you'll influence your friends, who might influence their friends. Hey! You could turn out to be an influencer after all!

PERSPECTIVE #6: DATE TO SERVE

Allow me to share a story. It's not a dating story. It's about another high-pressure social encounter: a job interview. And the story begins as I'm on the way to said interview.

The stakes were particularly high because I had to get a job before Julie and I could set a wedding date. That was my commitment to Julie's parents: the people I wanted to be *my* parents.

It was months since I had graduated from college, and Julie and I had been engaged for even longer, so I wanted this job. Badly.

Or did I? I was conflicted because on the one hand this interview was for just the sort of position I had prepared for in college. It was also with a well-known company. Plus, I just wanted a job so I could get married. (Did I mention that?)

On the other hand, without giving too many details, there were compromising positions I feared I might be put in working for this particular company. But I also wanted a job. You know, so I could get married.

In the car on the way to my appointment, I was mentally preparing for all one should expect to survive a job interview, while at the same time trying to figure out how I could make sure I wasn't signing a contract with the devil just so I could get a job and get married.

As I argued back and forth with myself, I sensed God's presence enter the car and tell me simply, "All you need to do is love, serve, and be a witness. I'll take care of the rest. I know if this is the job for you. You don't have to know all of that."

I've never forgotten that experience. Such a wave of peace rolled over me. A deep peace.

I went into that interview with a confidence that came from knowing God knew which job was right for me, so I didn't have to guess, and I didn't need to "make it happen." God would show me what I needed to know when I needed to know it. He would make whatever needed to happen, happen.

That left me with just three simple assignments which I had full control over:

- Seek to love those I interacted with by being patient, kind, gracious, and respectful

- Seek to serve those I interacted with by honoring their time and providing all the answers they wanted to know in both my résumé and interview

- Seek to witness to those I interacted with by being humble, but honest, about my values and convictions and the God who put them in my heart

Do you think these principles could work for you when you're stressed out on the way to your next date? I mean, assuming you get stressed out about that sort of thing.

A servant is only responsible for the work the master gives him to do. Our Master has told us all we need to know and all we need to do in any and every social situation: love, serve, and be a witness. He'll take care of the rest. He will handle the outcome.

So date to serve!

Follow Jesus's Great Example on Every Date

Everyone knows the great commandment. "And you shall love the Lord your God with all your heart and with all your soul and with all your mind and with all your strength … love your neighbor as yourself" (Mark 12:30-31 ESV). Jesus delivered these words back when His ministry was taking off.

Most are familiar with the great commission. "Go therefore and make disciples of all nations" (Matthew 28:19a ESV). Jesus shared this command after the triumph of His resurrection, right before He was taken up into heaven.

But on the night Jesus was betrayed, Jesus gave another "great" that isn't quite as well known: the great example of service.

Now before the Feast of the Passover, when Jesus knew that his hour had come to depart out of this world to the Father, having loved his own who were in the world, he loved them to the end. During supper, when the devil had already put it into the heart of Judas Iscariot, Simon's son, to betray him, Jesus, knowing that the Father had given all things into his hands, and that he had come from God and was going back to God, rose from supper. He laid aside his outer garments, and taking a towel, tied it around his waist. Then he poured water into a basin and began to wash the disciples' feet and to wipe them with the towel that was wrapped around him. —John 13:1-5 ESV

How could you "wash the feet" of those you dated?

It's not just a philosophical question, it's essential to living and dating as our Savior would have you live and date. We celebrate and honor Jesus' last supper every time we share communion, but we're called to imitate His life of service.

If I then, your Lord and Teacher, have washed your feet, you also ought to wash one another's feet. For I have given you an example, that you also should do just as I have done to you. Truly, truly, I say to you, a servant is not greater than his master, nor is a messenger greater than the one who sent him. If you know these things, blessed are you if you do them. —John 13:14-17 ESV

What if you dated like this? Date to serve!

PERSPECTIVE #7: DATE LIKE YOU'RE NEVER ALONE

Though God is our sole "Need-Meeter," He chooses to meet many of our needs in relationships. It has been this way since the creation of the first man. A relationship with God alone wasn't enough for Adam either. And, unlike us, he lived in a perfect paradise.

That said, if you don't understand the need God identified in Adam, you can wind up treating every person of the opposite sex like Adam did when he was tasked with naming every animal. "Are they 'the one'? Are they 'the one'? Are they 'the one'"?

However, if you rightly understand what Adam was missing apart from God, you can date like you're never alone!

What's Wrong with Being Alone?

On the third day, God created the earth and sea and saw it was good. Then He made the plants and trees and saw it was good. On the fourth day, He made the sun and moon: good. Fifth day: creatures which swam and flew: good. Sixth day: land animals: good.

But then God looked at Adam and said, "It is not good!"

Whaaaa? What went wrong? What wasn't good?

Complete the sentence: God said, "It is not good that the man should be …"

A. Celibate
B. Abstinent
C. Sexless
D. In possession of sexual needs with no legitimate outlet to meet them
E. None of the above

Of course, we all know God said it wasn't good for Adam to be "alone," but many of us sexualize this passage without realizing it.

The story is so familiar, and we already know where it's going. God's about to create Eve, the original "Whoa-man." God calls her Adam's "helper," but that must be code for "sex partner." After all, the first command God gives the original "first couple" is "be fruitful and multiply," which requires getting frisky, right?

However, God said it was not good for man to be alone, and believe it or not (and you really can't make this stuff up), the Hebrew word translated as "alone" is "bad." It is not good for Adam to be bad.

According to Strong's Concordance, "bad" is used in scripture to connotate the following meanings: alone, by itself, besides, apart, separation.

So instead of conveying the idea of a creature lacking romantic or sexual attachment, "bad" expresses the image of a body part being separated from the body or a tree branch being cut off from the tree.[7] A man without a girlfriend might be seen as pitiable to some, but a body part separated from the body has no purpose whatsoever. The same goes for a tree branch cut off from a tree.

In contrast, a body part connected to the body holds great significance. A hand, leg, or eye, in proper relationship to the body, enables the body to write, walk, or see. Indeed, every part of the body blesses the whole body as every part of the body is blessed by the whole body.

Likewise, a branch in proper relationship to the tree has great worth. The tree provides nutrients from the soil to the branch and in return the branch produces leaves, which turn light energy into chemical energy for the tree.

This is the need God had in mind when He said, "It is not good for man to be alone." It was not a sexual nor romantic need God identified but a relational one. He could see Adam needed to be in relationship with someone else, someone custom-made for him, like an arm needs a body, or a branch needs a tree.

This makes perfect sense when we remember that Adam was made in the image of a God who has eternally delighted in a relationship between three persons: Father, Son, and Spirit. Like God, Adam was created to delight in someone alike to himself and yet distinct from himself as the three persons

---

[7] "H905 - Bad - Strong's Hebrew Lexicon (KJV)." Blue Letter Bible, accessed May 12, 2022, https://www.blueletterbible.org/lexicon/h905/kjv/wlc/0-1/.

of the Trinity are one, but not the same as the other persons. As scripture puts it, "a helper fit for him." And what was true of Adam is true of you. It is not good for you to be alone.

Are You Really Alone without a Significant Other?

If we were created with a deep need for meaningful human connection, how can you date without the yearning, gnawing desperation to belong to a significant other?

You accomplish this by seeking that connection, not in the arms of some perfect "soul mate," but in community.

Start with your own family. If right away you're like, "Oh no! My family is crazy," I get it. Mine too.

But forget about the family I grew up with, you should see the family my children had to grow up in!

Are you getting what I'm saying? I'm not trying to be funny or self-effacing. I'm being honest. Everyone's family is crazy, flawed, disappointing, maybe even dysfunctional. However, everyone's family is also significant, precious, and—for better or for worse—an inescapable part of each of us.

Perhaps your family is so toxic you can't reconcile with anyone there.

If that is your story, I am truly sorry. However, you can't simply leave a toxic family background and waltz into the perfect marriage with the perfect person. You must deal with your past first, perhaps through counseling and therapy.

Many out there dating (or just waiting) seem to hope they'll wake up someday, like Adam, and discover God took one of their ribs while they were sleeping and formed the perfect person to end all their loneliness, heal all their brokenness, and ensure all their happiness.

Of course, that sort of worked for Adam, but we can't forget how Adam's "helper" wound up helping herself to that forbidden fruit. And now here we all are.

So, if you can't find the human connection you need in your family, and it's unrealistic to expect all those needs to be met by your future spouse, what are you to do?

Simply this: seek out a church family and get involved. Seek out wise mentors and same-gender friends, and be as intentional about growing those platonic relationships as you want to be in growing that perfect romance with the person of your dreams. Then, and only then, can you date like you're never alone. Because you won't be.

CHAPTER 14:

HOW TO KNOW IF YOU ARE RIGHT FOR EACH OTHER

If you desire to date in a healthy, whole way, more than confirming you like each other, you need to confirm you're *right* for each other. These fresh perspectives can empower you to date with that mindset. Speaking of mindset …

PERSPECTIVE #8: DATE WITH YOUR BRAIN

Dating to acquire and properly analyze the truth about your date requires that you date with your brain instead of your heart.

Now as soon as I bring up the word "analyze," I must concede it's quite common for many to analyze and even overanalyze a relationship to death instead of simply enjoying it.

However, most spend the majority of their analytical energy trying to discern their feelings and the feelings of the person they're interested in. They ask questions like, "Do I *like* them or do I *love* them?" or "Do they like me?" or "Is this true love?" or "Do they like *me* as much as I like *them*?"

Then after "confirming" their feelings, they make what seems to be the obvious right decisions about their relationship:

- "Oh! We both really like each other, so we should date seriously!"

- "Dang! I fear I like them way more than they like me,
  so I need to back out of this relationship before I get hurt."

- "They say they're not in love with me,
  but I'm going to change that!"

- "Whoa! They're coming on way too strong.
  Time for the 'friends' talk."

All these decisions are based on feelings. That probably doesn't sound troubling to you, but such analysis is often fruitless because feelings often defy analysis. Feelings are difficult to define or measure, and even once you do, they're subject to change. It's like trying to track the flight pattern of a dragonfly.

On the other hand, analyzing facts can lead you to make judgments which are more reliable.

- Either the person you're dating continues to prove faithful
  or not, kind or not, patient or not, humble or not.

- Either you can easily resolve conflict or you can't.

- Either communication comes naturally for the
  two of you or it doesn't.

- Either you share similar values and faith convictions
  or you don't.

So for certain, relationships are for analyzing, but spend more time analyzing facts than feelings. That's dating with your brain.

Beware of Infatuation

The main purpose of every date should be getting to know one another better. A little bit at a time.

Then you keep pursuing deeper relational intimacy until your analysis of the facts leads you to conclude that either the person you're dating is one of the nine strangers I warned you about in Chapters 4–6, or you're just not a good match.

If you reach either of those conclusions, you need to move on, regardless of what your feelings are telling you. Don't forget: feelings are always real, but they're not always right.

However, when you refuse to date with your brain and you insist on pursuing romance at all costs, you can be completely derailed from pursuing and growing in the knowledge of the person you're dating.

This is where the three laws of infatuation come into play.

Law #1: Infatuation is the goal of romance, not intimacy.

The whole romantic worldview is all about seeking out, submitting to, and celebrating the divine feeling of being "in love." This is why so many spend so much time analyzing their feelings and the feelings of their love interest.

We already explained the impermanent nature of limerence in Chapter 12, but while you are under the influence of its temporary reign you can believe many things that are not true. The lies of limerence include the following:

- **You have never felt this way before** (not even all those other times you fell in love with other people).

- **No one else has ever felt this way before** (not even those who claim they have).

- **This is fate** (so you can't help how you feel, or they feel, or even control what those feelings lead either of you to do).

Believing those lies gives full control of your dating life over to your feelings, as it denies any control to your brain. You will ignore red flags, rush the relationship, and make increasingly imprudent choices as you ignore and even resent the advice of those who know you best and love you most.

However, the reality is that almost everyone has experienced that "madly in love" feeling at least once, if not multiple times, because the feelings of limerence are common to man. It's part of what makes being crazy in love so … ah … crazy.

Dr. Joe Beam, sexologist, introduced me to this concept of limerence, describing situations where a married man in love with another woman will declare he has never felt for his wife the feelings which he shares for this new woman.

The wife can even produce love letters her husband wrote to her expressing all the exact same feelings that her husband now claims for this new woman. Still, he will swear he didn't know what he was talking about when he wrote those letters to his wife.[8]

You see the irony, right?

The husband can believe with all his heart he didn't know what he was talking about when he was in love with his wife. He might even declare he never really loved her at all!

At the same time, he can be certain—dead certain—the feelings he is experiencing now for this new woman are true love. He might even feel it ignoble to deny his new feelings.

Essentially, the person in the throes of limerence will rewrite history to fit the narrative they want to believe in the moment.

---

[8] Joe Beam, *"I'm In Love with Another; What Should I Do?"* crosswalk.com, December 12, 2011, https://www.crosswalk.com/family/marriage/i-m-in-love-with-another-man.html.

I hope this scares you the way it should. Your feelings are not to be trusted! Feelings are not necessarily false, they are always information, but they should be corroborated with facts. Especially when you're making decisions that could impact your future.

Law #2: Infatuation is easier to grow than intimacy.

Intimacy is something you have to build and requires the following elements:

1. **Intimacy requires time.** Truly getting to know someone always takes time. If you try to build intimacy too quickly, bad things often happen.

2. **Intimacy requires understanding.** To know someone deeply almost calls for a level of knowledge akin to learning a new language.

3. **Intimacy requires intentionality.** You can become familiar with someone over time without much effort, but knowing someone deeply is something you must be deliberate about.

4. **Intimacy requires vulnerability.** A counselor or therapist may hold intimate knowledge about you, but you do not share an intimate relationship with them because intimacy necessitates vulnerability from all participants in the relationship. It's an "all skate."

In stark contrast, infatuation requires none of those things.

1. **Infatuation takes no time at all.** You can fall in love in an instant. That's why they call it "falling in love," or "love at first sight."

2. **Infatuation takes no understanding.** It defies understanding. This is why someone who has fallen in love might describe it this way: "I didn't even know what hit me!" (Because they really didn't.)

3. **Infatuation takes no intentionality.** People will say, "I can't choose who I love," but what they really are describing is how infatuation seems to choose us.

4. **Infatuation takes no vulnerability.** In fact, you can be head over heels for someone who's head over heels for you and neither of you even know the other's name.

Important note about that last point: Though it requires no vulnerability to enjoy infatuation, it can make you very, very vulnerable. In fact, you can wind up sharing things with someone you're in love with that you haven't even shared with your closest friends. Add alcohol to the mix, and there can be no secrets left to tell.

Further, this sort of sharing can intensify your feelings of closeness. Indeed, social scientists have researched the effect of secret-sharing.[9] They have conducted studies where they encourage pairs of strangers to share a secret with each other. Invariably, they discovered this exercise dramatically increases feelings of closeness between every couple. Just one secret!

How does infatuation tempt us to such imprudent vulnerability? That leads us to the third law of infatuation.

Law #3: Infatuation will prevent you from growing in intimacy as it deadens your need for intimacy.

You've probably heard someone say something like, "I know we only just met last night, but I feel like I've known them my whole life."

Sentiments like this make many swoon and others gag, but it makes me see red flags waving in the gale-force winds of infatuation.

---

[9] Mariela E. Jaffé and Maria Douneva, *"[PDF] Secretive and Close? How Sharing Secrets May Impact Perceptions of Distance: Semantic Scholar,"* undefined, January 1, 1970, https://www.semanticscholar.org/paper/Secretive-and-close-How-sharing-secrets-may-impact-Jaff%C3%A9-Douneva/d65fb0ead2844a00c3c597f80d05de58203185df.

Why? Because if you already feel like you've known someone your whole life, then what's left to get to know? In other words, *feeling* like you already know someone can easily slide into *believing and acting* like you already know them.

You might as well get married! And some do!! (And that's another reason why we have divorce.)

Even if infatuation doesn't tempt you to that level of imprudence, feeling like you already know someone will frequently keep you from asking the hard questions necessary to discern the true health of both the person you're dating and the relationship you share.

However, the truth will come out eventually. Better to happen after the first month or even the first year of dating than after the first month of marriage. So I urge you again, date with your brain!

Suppression Leads to Obsession

So how do you go about dating while holding your emotions in check?

Here's what not to do. Don't attempt to suppress your feelings. In other words, don't try to stuff them down, bury them, or forget about them. This simply doesn't work, at least not in the long run because suppression often leads to obsession.

Example: What's the first thing you think about when I tell you NOT to think about a pink elephant?

In the same way, trying to tell yourself, *Don't think about last night,* or *Don't think about how gorgeous they are,* or *Don't think about tomorrow night's date,* will do nothing to help you moderate your emotions.

The more you tell yourself to ignore the feelings of romance, the more you will fixate on those feelings. But not only is suppressing your feelings as futile as trying to ignore a pink elephant in the room, it's a terribly unhealthy pattern for dealing with your emotions, even if you're good at suppressing them. And some people are very good at it. Psychopaths and serial killers for instance.

Instead of suppressing, I urge you to supplant your feelings with facts. Instead of attempting to just bury your feelings, supplanting begins with digging up those feelings—and dealing with them—and then replacing them with relevant facts.

For instance, let your feelings about your partner's appearance inspire you to do some soul searching with questions like these:

- How much is my interest in them based on their appearance?

- What do I like so much about their appearance, and what does that say about what I value and prioritize?

- If they were in an accident and were disfigured, would I still enjoy being with them and desire being close to them? Why or why not?

- Is their appearance blinding me to any obvious character flaws or relational conflict?

- What are their top five character strengths and how have they proven them?

- What are their top five character weaknesses and how have they demonstrated their awareness of them and their commitment to working on them?

Will this process of questioning kill the power of infatuation? Well, no, not totally. But with every question posed, pondered, and answered, you move more from feelings to facts, as you pursue true intimacy over infatuation. That's called dating with your brain!

PERSPECTIVE #9: DATE TO ENJOY VERBAL INTERCOURSE

If a life-giving, lifelong marriage is not something you desire, or if it's something you desire but doubt you will ever enjoy, then the temptation to submit to your sexual passions can be nearly impossible to ignore.

However, if you believe in marriage, if marriage is not only something you desire and believe you can attain, but believe it is a mission you're likely called to, then you have much to lose by engaging in premarital sexual intimacy. If marriage is your goal, then you need to focus all of your pursuit of intimacy on the conversational kind and engage in as much verbal intercourse as you can!

Why Verbal and Sexual Intercourse Don't Mix

Let's be honest here. Once you've held hands for the first time with someone you are crazy about, you want to hold hands all the time. And once you've kissed for the first time, you want to kiss more often, and longer, and with more than your lips. And then you want to kiss more than each other's lips. Like elbows.

Bottom line, once you've begun to engage in romantic or sexual intimacy in any form, it has the tendency of taking over the relationship. So eros love doesn't only compellingly draw you downstream toward the waterfall of sexual bliss, it also tends to rapidly overflow its banks, flooding other parts of your relationship.

In other words, there's an opportunity cost for every decision we make.

The True Opportunity Cost of Making Out

There's an opportunity cost to spending your dating life pursuing physical intimacy; even if you keep your make-out sessions PG-13. Or even PG! If you're not familiar with the concept, an "opportunity cost" is an economic term which recognizes the loss of benefits that takes place whenever you make a choice. Namely, making any particular choice in the moment means the following:

1. You must forgo all other opportunities in that moment of decision.

2. You must forgo all the potential benefits you could have derived from taking advantage of those other opportunities in that moment.

This is the economic science behind the fear of missing out. It's what keeps you from committing to a Bible study in case you might get an invite to a party the same night. It's what keeps you from making up your mind at a new restaurant with a big menu. It's what keeps you from deciding to pursue a dating relationship with one person, when there are so many other persons of interest in your life.

So if you are determined to go with the inevitable flow of physical intimacy—even if you stop before you "go too far"—what's the opportunity cost? Think about it. While you're exploring your date's body, what are you *not* doing?

You're not growing in the knowledge of your date's soul. That's who they truly are! Not a hot body filled with hormones, but a sacred soul filled with hopes, fears, dreams, regrets, joys, and sorrows. We're talking about the part of a person that can grow more bold and beautiful with age, while time and gravity take their toll on the body.

Now if you're sexually involved, making out, or simply madly in love with someone, you may already feel like you are soul mates, but a soul isn't something you feel, it's something you know. So date to enjoy verbal intercourse!

PERSPECTIVE #10: DATE IN THE DELIGHT OF YOUR FIRST LOVE

Can you remember when the love of God first broke through to you? When He "found you" (without even having to look for you because He has always known where you were every moment of your life)? Can you remember a time when His love was so real you couldn't help but respond in passionate obedience?

If not, I am compelled to suggest you may not know the God of the Bible because He's unimaginably good! He is perfect, infinite, and unchanging, and so is the marvelously extravagant love He delights to lavish on those who, apart from His grace and mercy, would be worthy of no love at all.

But if you do know this God and His love, can I ask you a question? Has your passion for Him died down a bit? Or a lot?

Perhaps you're still "living for Him," even striving valiantly to do so, but more out of duty than desire. If so, you might relate to this description of the church at Ephesus:

> *I know your deeds and your labor and perseverance, and that*
> *you cannot tolerate evil people, and you have put those who call*
> *themselves apostles to the test, and they are not, and you found them*
> *to be false; and you have perseverance and have endured on account*
> *of My name, and have not become weary.* —Revelation 2:2–3 NASB

The above words are not only affirming, they are some of the very few affirming words Jesus has to share with any of the seven churches He addresses in Revelation. In other words, this church is doing the right things!

Maybe you feel that way with dating. Perhaps Jesus would say these words to you:

> *I know your [dating practices] and your labor and perseverance,*
> *and that you cannot [go out with] evil people, and you have put*
> *to the test those who call themselves [dating candidates], and they*
> *are not, and you found them to be [Mr./Ms. Wrongs you shouldn't*
> *date]; and you have perseverance and have endured on account*
> *of My name, and have not become weary [in your singleness].*
> —Revelation 2:2-3 NASB (sans bracketed edits)

If you're feeling that, here's what God had to say to the church at Ephesus. And you.

> *But I have this against you, that you have left your first love.*
> *Therefore, remember from where you have fallen, and repent,*
> *and do the deeds you did at first; or else I am coming to you and*
> *I will remove your lampstand from its place—unless you repent.*
> —Revelation 2:4–5 NASB

Essentially God is saying, "You're doing the right things, but you're doing it wrong!" Because doing all the right things doesn't impress God. It doesn't even please God. Obedience out of love is what the Father desires: a love rooted in faith.

> *And without faith it is impossible to please him, for whoever would*
> *draw near to God must believe that he exists and that he rewards*
> *those who seek him.* —Hebrews 11:6 ESV

And so our final perspective on dating to change your relationship life is also a command. It's a command coming from Your God who loves You, so that You could love Him. Date in the delight of your first love!

What If God Turns Out to Be Who You Believe Him to Be?

Do you remember Jesus' parable of the servants who were each given talents before their Master departed on a long journey?

In that tale, we can learn something very important about the connection between trust, obedience, and delighting or abiding in God's love.

> *For it will be like a man going on a journey, who called his servants*
> *and entrusted to them his property. To one he gave five talents, to*
> *another two, to another one, to each according to his ability. Then*
> *he went away. He who had received the five talents went at once*
> *and traded with them, and he made five talents more. So also he*

who had the two talents made two talents more. But he who had received the one talent went and dug in the ground and hid his master's money. —Matthew 25:14-18 ESV

Two servants invested the talents they received. One hid them. What made the difference between those who took action and the one who did not?

Now after a long time the master of those servants came and settled accounts with them. And he who had received the five talents came forward, bringing five talents more, saying, 'Master, you delivered to me five talents; here, I have made five talents more.' His master said to him, 'Well done, good and faithful servant. You have been faithful over a little; I will set you over much. Enter into the joy of your master.' And he also who had the two talents came forward, saying, 'Master, you delivered to me two talents; here, I have made two talents more.' His master said to him, 'Well done, good and faithful servant. You have been faithful over a little; I will set you over much. Enter into the joy of your master.'
—Matthew 25:19-23 ESV

Not a lot of hints as to the motives of the industrious servants, but it's clear they trusted the Master would deal fairly with them. And, in the end, He did even better. He dealt *bountifully* with them. Now let's listen to the response of the third servant.

He also who had received the one talent came forward, saying, 'Master, I knew you to be a hard man, reaping where you did not sow, and gathering where you scattered no seed, so I was afraid, and I went and hid your talent in the ground. Here, you have what is yours.' —Matthew 25:24-25 ESV

We could say a lot about the third servant—none of it good—but what is clear: he most certainly did *not* trust the master.

But his master answered him, 'You wicked and slothful servant!
You knew that I reap where I have not sown and gather where I
scattered no seed? Then you ought to have invested my money with
the bankers, and at my coming I should have received what was
my own with interest.' —Matthew 25:26-27 ESV

Two servants believed the Master to be trustworthy, and the Master proved to be so … to them. One servant believed the Master to be hard—other translations say "difficult to please" or "unscrupulous"—and the Master proved to be so … to him. However, we know from the first two servants that if the third had trusted the Master as well, His blessing awaited him.

So who do you believe our Master to be?

Without faith, it is impossible to please Him! Will you trust Him? Then you will obey Him like the two servants. And then you will rest in His love. You will "enter into the joy of the Master," and you will be able to date in the delight of your first love!

The Secret to Trusting God

Do you want to trust God like the first two servants but just don't feel like you can? Then you will find it almost impossible to obey God. Just like the third servant.

Who could blame you? We generally don't obey people we don't trust. Unless we think we have to, but then that's obedience out of fear.

There is no fear in love, but perfect love casts out fear. For fear has
to do with punishment, and whoever fears has not been perfected
in love. We love because he first loved us. —1 John 4:18-19 ESV

So how can you learn to trust God so you can obey Him? The very same way God has always encouraged His people to trust Him. He asks us to remember who He is and what He has done for us in the past. Actually, He *commands* us to remember. And sternly warns us not to forget.

> *And when the Lord your God brings you into the land that he swore to your fathers, to Abraham, to Isaac, and to Jacob, to give you—with great and good cities that you did not build, and houses full of all good things that you did not fill, and cisterns that you did not dig, and vineyards and olive trees that you did not plant— and when you eat and are full, then* **take care lest you forget the Lord***, who brought you out of the land of Egypt, out of the house of slavery. It is the Lord your God you shall fear. Him you shall serve and by his name you shall swear.* —Deuteronomy 6:10-13 ESV (emphasis mine)

We have even *more* reason than the Israelites to remember what God has done for us. He died for us! We have even *more* reason to remember how great our God is. He didn't just demonstrate signs and wonders, He rose from the dead.

If you have followed God for some time, odds are there are personal ways He's proven His love for you. Remember! Take the time to recall His mighty works in your life.

Or maybe you don't yet have personal accounts of God's faithfulness. Not only is there the testimony of the scriptures, but there are the testimonies of the saints in the church today who declare our God reigns and is worthy of our trust and obedience! Then you can truly surrender your life to Him and obey Him. Even in your dating life. *Especially* in your dating life!

Trust and obey. Remember and surrender. To help you internalize these four objectives in order, consider this simple diagram.

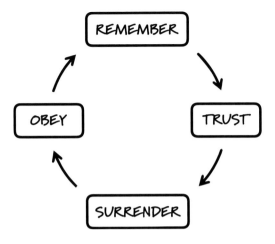

Let this be your template for dating in the delight of your First Love!

This chapter marks the end
of the fifth lesson in an 8-week
LoveEd study. For discussion questions
and resources go to:

FMUniversity.net/DatePrep-wk5

CHAPTER 15:
HOW TO KNOW YOU'RE READY TO DATE

I have been asked many times if I had any doubts standing at the altar on my wedding day, and I always give the same answer.

"Absolutely not. And emphatically yes."

What I mean is that on the one hand I had no doubts about the person I was choosing to marry. I knew Julie wasn't perfect, but I knew we were a good match.

Of course, many, souped up on the brain chemistry of limerence, stand at the altar with no doubts, even as innumerable red flags flap fanatically in the winds of impending doom. However, I had known my bride as a good friend for over two years, as a girlfriend for one year, and as a fiancé for another year. As our own relationship grew, I watched Julie grow in personal maturity in her relationships with others and in her relationship with the Lord. In addition, I also had the firm affirmation and full support of the family and friends who knew me best and loved me most. And she did as well.

However, while I had no doubts about who I was marrying, I had significant doubts about the institution of marriage itself. Not that I suspected there was something wrong with marriage, but that I feared marriage might reveal there was something wrong with me. And that this might even be part of the reason for marriage: revealing my true self, in all its disappointing imperfections.

By our wedding day, I had read enough in marriage books and learned enough through personal observation to know marriage would not be everything I hoped it would be. I knew marriage was good, but in the way that medicine is good. Not in the way that tacos are good. And so, I thought it possible that I might one day regret marrying at all.

However, I knew God had been an integral part of our relationship. He walked with us as we walked together. I knew He would continue to walk with us as we walked together, for He promised never to leave us nor forsake us!

And so, ultimately, my confidence came from the Lord because I knew that even if the day arrived when I regretted vowing to live the rest of my life for the good of another, God's power would be sure enough, His wisdom sound enough, and His grace sweet enough to carry us through any drought or storm. And it has been.

It is one of my greatest hopes for you that you will one day stand at the altar with no doubt about the wisdom of your marital choice, in spite of the sober reality that you don't know the future. And you will hold this peace because ultimately your confidence won't be in the person you're marrying or the future you don't know but in our God who does know the future and will carry you through together.

> *Now may the God of peace himself sanctify you completely, and may your whole spirit and soul and body be kept blameless at the coming of our Lord Jesus Christ. He who calls you is faithful; he will surely do it.* —1 Thessalonians 5:23-24 ESV

PREREQUISITES FOR ROMANCE 101

I want you to be able to stand at the altar with no doubts—at least none of the wrong kind of doubts—so I want to empower you to date with confidence and prudence. If you personally resonate with that desire, then you need to look at the next part of our definition for friends-first dating; the part about growing a friendship.

> **Friends-First Dating:** Intentional time invested in one other person **for the purpose of growing a friendship** that might lead to a life-giving, lifelong marriage

Again, the purpose of friends-first dating is not marriage. Marriage is the goal. The purpose is "growing a friendship," because If you want to share the kind of well-founded confidence Julie and I enjoyed on our wedding day, you want to first grow the kind of friendship Julie and I grew long before our wedding day.

But to grow that kind of friendship you need to possess a certain level of relational maturity, so in this chapter and the two that follow we'll share six prerequisites for Romance 101.

Of course, no one wants to be told they're not mature enough to date, but the reality is that most out there dating are *not* mature enough to date. And that's another reason why we have divorce.

If you realize you're not ready, you've discovered something many never discover and suffer accordingly. In the end, the truth will set you free because the truth can move you to make the personal adjustments necessary to enter (or reenter) the dating world with competence and confidence! Sound good? Then here we go!

PREREQUISITE #1: YOU HABITUALLY HONOR YOUR PARENTS

Wondering what your relationship with your parents has to do with dating?

First, let's address what honoring your parents has to do with success in life in general, because the sacred little secret of the ten commandments is that there's only one commandment with a promise:

> *Honor your father and your mother,* **that your days may be long in the land that the Lord your God is giving you.**
> —Exodus 20:12 ESV (emphasis mine)

> *Honor your father and your mother, as the Lord your God commanded you,* **that your days may be long, and that it may go well with you in the land that the Lord your God is giving you.** —Deuteronomy 5:16 ESV (emphasis mine)

And Paul made it clear that the Old Testament promise still applies today!

> *Children, obey your parents in the Lord, for this is right. "Honor your father and mother"* **(this is the first commandment with a promise)**, *"that it may go well with you and that you may live long in the land."* —Ephesians 6:1-3 ESV (emphasis mine)

Scripture tells us that our relationship with our parents will powerfully impact our life overall. For those who put more stock in science than Scripture, ask any experienced counselor, therapist, or life coach, and they'll tell you the same thing.

Now, do you have to keep obeying your parents after you're living on your own as an adult? No, the command is to "honor" our parents, something any child can do at any age. And according to this passage, something every child *should* do at *every* age.

What Honoring Your Parents Does *Not* Mean

In addition to obeying your parents in everything for the rest of your life, here's what honoring your parents is *not*:

- Agreeing with them about everything
- Always trying to make them happy
- Never having any conflict with them
- Enabling them to continue in destructive habits and relational patterns
- Being the perfect angel
- Pretending they were the perfect parents

What Honoring Your Parents Does Mean

- Respecting their authority, experience, perspective
- Seeking their best interests
- Striving to live at peace with them
- Granting grace and thinking the best of them
- Confessing your offenses against them
- Forgiving their offenses against you

What If You Took God at His Word?

Truth is, most of us have been wounded the most by those who owed us the most: our parents. So, the command to honor them may come across to many as absurd, to others as cruel, to some as both.

But something you should remember about God is that He is a good Father who doesn't ask His children to obey cruel and absurd commands.

Might the task seem impossible? Indeed! God is famous for calling His people to seemingly impossible tasks, with Scripture replete with historical accounts of how God does the impossible Himself through His people.

But, my friend, let's lift our eyes from the task at hand and consider the reward!

Let's take God at His word. If you learn to honor your parents, good will follow. Who wouldn't want this sort of blessing as they navigate their dating life? Wouldn't you?

Confessions of a Father Who Failed

Can I be honest with you for a minute? Really honest?

I am a dad who has failed all five of my children in various ways over my twenty-six years of parenting so far. That said, I've confessed my sins to them sincerely, specifically, and repeatedly. But the scars still remain. In some cases, the hurt still remains.

I've no doubt your own parents failed you. Maybe criminally. And perhaps, adding insult to injury, they've never confessed and repented.

It's easy to think, "If they were truly sorry, I could forgive them," but let me assure you, while reconciliation requires the confession and repentance of your offender (and time to reestablish trust), forgiveness of the sins committed against you is your task alone.

Your willingness to forgive says nothing at all about your offender. It says everything about you.

However, in the hopes of helping you forgive, consider this: until you've been a parent yourself for a couple decades, you really can't imagine how difficult it is to be a parent.

No, you really can't. I realize from your perspective it may not seem that hard, but I'm urging you to look at life from *your parent's* perspective. And then realize that unless you're raising children the same age as you (which, though I'm not a biologist, I believe is a medical impossibility), you can't even comprehend their perspective because you've never been there.

Meanwhile, though you may feel they don't understand you (and they may not), your parents have actually been your age at one time—for an entire year. In fact, they've already spent a full year being the age you are about to turn, and so on.

Yes, I realize it's a different world you're growing up in than the world your parents grew up in. It's also a different world they're parenting in.

Look, I'm not trying to justify your parents. I'm simply urging you to accept the reality that you can't imagine how hard it is to parent. It makes adulting look like a cakewalk holding hands with your favorite social media influencer.

If you can live in this reality, you have a far better chance of forgiving your parents. In doing so, you will not only honor your parents, you will set yourself free of the bitterness that would sabotage all your important relationships. Even your dating relationships. *Especially* your dating relationships!

The Practical Reason to Honor Your Parents

Consider these deep questions:

- Do you want to be ready to forgive the people who will hurt you in the future? Or would you rather compile a lifelong list of people you no longer speak to (or speak of)?

- Do you want to be adept at empathizing with the people you're closest to? Or would you rather spend your relational energy trying to get everyone else to empathize with you?

- Do you want to be skilled at conflict resolution? Or would you rather avoid conflict as best you can until you have no other option but to come out with both guns blazing?

- Do you want to be the kind of person who can freely accept and appreciate those who are different from you without compromising your own identity? Or would you rather be the person who is always right or always changing to survive your environment?

What's the point of this interrogation? I'm simply pointing out that honoring your parents is not just a spiritual promise, it's a practical reality. Check it out!

- In learning to forgive offenses of your parents, you prepare yourself to forgive others.

- In learning to empathize with your parents, you become adept at empathizing with others.

- In learning to deal with family conflict, you learn to deal with conflict with others.

- In learning to accept differences in your parents, while remaining true to who you are, you become the kind of person who can accept the differences in others without losing your identity.

You see, God didn't give you a family to torture you but to teach you. He didn't give you parents to make you miserable but to make you mature.

Can you see how this would empower you to date in a whole and healthy way, while preparing you for a life-giving, lifelong marriage?

PREREQUISITE #2: YOU KNOW HOW TO MAKE PEACE

You might be tempted to associate the idea of making peace with dying, like before you go, you want to make peace with your loved ones. However, do these words from the Apostle Paul read like they were written to people who are about to die?

> ***Live in harmony*** *with one another. Do not be haughty, but associate with the lowly. Never be wise in your own sight. Repay no one evil for evil, but give thought to do what is honorable in the sight of all. If possible, so far as it depends on you,* ***live peaceably*** *with all. Beloved, never avenge yourselves, but leave it to the wrath of God, for it is written, "Vengeance is mine,*

> *I will repay, says the Lord." To the contrary, "if your enemy is*
> *hungry, feed him; if he is thirsty, give him something to drink;*
> *for by so doing you will heap burning coals on his head."*
> *Do not be overcome by evil, but overcome evil with good.*
> —Romans 12:16-21 ESV (emphasis mine)

Based on these instructions, I suggest making peace is less about dying well and more about living well. Why wait?

The reason peacemaking is so critical is because conflict is so common. You just can't get around it. Conflict is an unavoidable fact of life. There's a reason why scripture is filled with admonitions like the words above from Romans 12.

But while we often associate conflict with difficult relationships and difficult people, conflict can rear its ugly head in even the best of relationships where you want to see eye to eye, like in a dating relationship you hope will lead to a life-giving, lifelong marriage. So, if you have established the pattern of terminating and moving on from difficult relationships, I urge you to consider whether you're ready to date.

The Golden Rule Isn't Only for People You Like

Do unto others as you would have them do unto you. The golden rule comes straight from the mouth of Jesus in Luke 6:31, and most agree it's a great way to live. But do you know the context in which those words were shared? Here are the four verses that precede everyone's favorite rule.

> *But I say to you who hear, Love your **enemies**, do good to **those***
> ***who hate you**, bless **those who curse you**, pray for **those who***
> ***abuse you**. To one who strikes you on the cheek, offer the other also,*
> *and from one who takes away your cloak do not withhold your*
> *tunic either. Give to everyone who begs from you, and from one*
> *who takes away your goods do not demand them back. And as you*

wish that others would do to you, do so to them. —Luke 6:27-31 ESV (emphasis mine)

Little known fact about the good ol' golden rule was that it was never about how we should treat our friends or even people in general. It's specifically addressing how we should treat our enemies. The golden rule is merely a summary of the detailed directions given previously in how to deal with difficult people.

What should you do to your enemies who hate you, curse you, and abuse you? You should love them, do good to them, bless them, and pray for them.

Clear? Yes. Simple? No.

That said, if Jesus commands us to treat our enemies this way, how much more should we treat our friends and loved ones who he's put in our lives, not to beat us down, but to build us up into the image of Christ?

The Blessing in Peacemaking

More than just being called to make peace, we are called to be peacemakers, so peace is more about being than doing!

> *Blessed are the peacemakers, for they will be called sons of God.* —Matthew 5:9 NASB

But again, just like the commandment to honor your parents, the call to live at peace comes with a pretty phenomenal promise which Jesus mentions in Luke 6, shortly after the instructions we quoted above from verses 27–31.

> *But love your enemies, and do good, and lend, expecting nothing in return, and **your reward will be great, and you will be sons of the Most High**, for he is kind to the ungrateful and the evil. Be merciful, even as your Father is merciful.* —Luke 6:35-36 ESV (emphasis mine)

Why Seek Peace, Even if You Can't Find It

I don't know about you, but I'm the kind of guy who doesn't want to try something unless I think I can succeed.

However, you can't really approach peacemaking from this perspective, or you'll never try it. Or if you do make the attempt, you won't keep at it for long because true peace requires reconciliation. That is where two or more parties get along together, which means reconciliation entails effort on the part of all parties involved. Otherwise, you cannot successfully enjoy peace in that relationship.

But let's say you are like me, and if you can't win, you don't want to play. If you expend enormous energy toward seeking peace but can't find it, what can you succeed at? What's in it for you?

Simply this: pleasing our God! In fact, we can faithfully honor Him in a relationship, even if peace remains ever elusive.

Remember, there is a blessing in seeking peace. It may not be a blessing we're promised in this life (like the blessing we're promised for honoring our parents), but know this for certain: no one will be disappointed by eternal blessings.

> *Blessed are those who are persecuted for righteousness' sake, for theirs is the kingdom of heaven. Blessed are you when others revile you and persecute you and utter all kinds of evil against you falsely on my account. Rejoice and be glad, for your reward is great in heaven, for so they persecuted the prophets who were before you.*
> —Matthew 5:10-12 ESV

The Only Source of Peace

You still may not be convinced. Why try this peacemaking thing, if the work is so hard and the effort often unfruitful? Because ultimately, peace doesn't come from pleasing other people. And it doesn't come from pleasing yourself. It comes from pleasing God.

> *Rejoice in the Lord always; again I will say, rejoice. Let your reasonableness be known to everyone. The Lord is at hand; do not be anxious about anything, but in everything by prayer and supplication with thanksgiving let your requests be made known to God. And the peace of God, which surpasses all understanding, will guard your hearts and your minds in Christ Jesus.* —Philippians 4:4-7 ESV

I can tell you I have known this peace many times in the midst of terribly broken relationships. I know this peace even now, and it is wonderful!

Would I prefer all my important relationships to be healthy, whole, and free of misunderstanding, disappointment, and conflict? YES! But again, there is no peace apart from Christ.

That isn't just a nice spiritual thing to say, it is an absolutely essential reality for you to live in if you expect to thrive in marriage. There are going to be times—perhaps whole seasons—where you aren't going to find the peace you long for in your marriage. You may have already known times living in the family you have grown up with where peace was nowhere to be found.

Ultimately, peace only comes from God. Sometimes He gives us peace through a friend, a pet, a beautiful day, a latte, or a spouse. But know this for certain: peace was never actually in the friend, the pet, the day, or the latte. And the peace will not be in the spouse. Peace is always from Him and only found in Him.

> *I have said these things to you, that in me you may have peace. In the world you will have tribulation. But take heart; I have overcome the world.* —John 16:33 ESV

We can forget this truth when we grow accustomed to finding peace in our circumstances, people, or whatever, but God will not let anything—even *good* things—become idols we look to for our peace.

So, learn to seek peace in Christ alone, and you will learn to be the peacemaker He made you to be. Then, and only then, can you experience peace in your dating life, no matter your relationship status.

CHAPTER 16:
ARE YOU RATIONAL, OR DO YOU RATIONALIZE?

In one of our LoveEd classes, I asked students what they wanted from their future spouse. We quickly had a whiteboard filled with important character qualities and relationship benefits:

- acceptance
- to be loved
- trust
- kindness
- attraction
- sex
- respect
- chemistry
- inside jokes
- honesty
- shared history
- connection
- maturity
- understanding
- reliability

That's just a fraction of all they came up with, but you get the idea. Then I asked each student to pick the one item from our list that was the most important to them.

Of course, one of the students picked "sex." Not seriously, of course. But maybe a little.

Another student was more thoughtful. They picked "maturity." They reasoned that maturity would guarantee most of the other important qualities/benefits on the list. A mature person would be appropriately accepting, loving, trusting, kind, reliable, respectable, honest, etc. Completely rational, right?

But the truth? When it comes to dating, many of us—dare I say the majority—will overlook a mature person because of a lack of physical attraction, an attribute that delivers none of the other important character qualities or relationship benefits on the list above.

And even worse? Many more will *ignore* a glaring lack of maturity because of an overpowering physical attraction. As the heart is carried away on the wings of emotion, the brain will begin churning out the rationalizations.

- *"They're not that bad!"* Oh, what a relief! Admittedly, they're bad, but they could be worse. They could be a serial killer. Are they a serial killer?

- *"They have a really good heart."* If that's so, why doesn't that heart demonstrate its "goodness" more often? And in more ways?

- *"But they're so sweet to me!"* As if any jerk doesn't know how to be sweet to somebody for whom they have romantic feelings (as long as those feelings last) or from whom they want something (like the aforementioned sex).

Those kinds of rationalizations are crazy, aren't they? And yet so common, but if you want to avoid as much heartbreak, rejection, and regret as you can, you need to learn to date less emotionally and more rationally. Which means you need to grow relationally. With that in mind, here are our next two prerequisites for Romance 101.

PREREQUISITE #3: YOU HAVE GENUINE SAME-GENDER FRIENDSHIPS

Nate Larkin, with the Samson Society recovery ministry, once told me, "We all have same-sex needs. They're just not sexual."

Timeless truth, brilliantly stated. We all need friends with whom we can share deep relational intimacy without any of the complications that romantic or sexual attraction bring to a relationship.

However, we often don't recognize our need for friends like we recognize our desire for romance. And more often than not, many of us believe we already have our "same-sex needs" met when we really don't. In other words, we have friends—perhaps a lot of them—but not the kind who truly know us deeply.

So what happens? We take our God-given desire for marriage and add to it our God-given need to be known and loved on the level of genuine friendship, and we look for someone to date. And no one—not even "the one"—will ever be able to fill all of our needs for intimacy.

That said, if your desire for a significant other is raging out of control like a wildfire of passion, allow me to suggest that maybe your "same-sex needs" aren't being met.

Changing Focus from Girlfriend to Guy Friends

Largely ignorant of healthy dating practices, I arrived on campus my freshman year of college determined to identify and secure my first girlfriend. And for a minute, I thought I had!

Jenny (name changed to protect the innocent) was absolutely gorgeous, positively hilarious, insanely intelligent, and on fire for Jesus. She accepted my date invite to the homecoming dance, which I rapped to her like Vanilla Ice in the middle of Itza Pizza in the Student Union Building. Just like a movie, right? Plus, we had already begun getting to know each other as friends (as best you can in the first month and a half of school), and we really seemed to get along.

The night of homecoming, I took her out for dinner in a friend's red convertible Cadillac—complete with car phone—and as I remember, we had a fabulous evening together and with friends.

But sometime after homecoming, she seemed to get cold feet. Probably because that "insanely intelligent" part of her was sensing things were moving way too fast. Because they were.

In retrospect, I realize that in my first semester of college, I was driven as much by my same-sex needs as I was by my desire for a girlfriend because I was a guy who had never truly grown deep same-gender friendships in my life. I didn't even know they were a thing!

Fortunately, as the fear of getting the "let's just be friends" talk caused me to pump the brakes on my pursuit of Jenny, I was at the same time making friends with a few fabulous guys, beginning with the first accountability partners of my life: Yancey and Pete.

I shared with them my high school struggle with pornography and my dreams for what I wanted to do with my life after college. They shared their lives with me honestly and freely. So, perhaps for the first time in my life, I was getting my same-sex needs met. And as I did, I dialed back my desperation for a girlfriend from boil to simmer.

Don't get me wrong. I still wanted a girlfriend. If I didn't, I wouldn't have gone out with over thirty different girls my freshman year. However, though my motives for dating weren't entirely healthy, at least I wasn't driven to find "the one" like I was when I arrived at school. I had a community of friends who could tell me I was alright, even if some girl didn't like me back. And the longer I attended college, the more that community both expanded and deepened.

I would like to see you date with this same sense of peace. Wouldn't you?

First Come the Groomsmen and Then Comes the Bride!

Essentially, what I'm suggesting with this "same-gender friend" prerequisite is a paradigm shift when it comes to building your future wedding party:

- A man should seek out his groomsmen before looking for his bride.

- A woman should seek out her bridesmaids before looking for her groom.

To be clear:

DON'T: Ask people to be in your wedding if you don't have someone to marry first.

DO: Seek to identify and build relationships with friends who could wholeheartedly affirm and support you and your marriage on your wedding day.

Rather Hang Out with the Other Gender?

What if you more easily relate to those of the gender that is not your own? What if you actually find it rather difficult to grow close friendships with those of your same gender?

This was true of me prior to college for at least two reasons:

1. I was a guy with absolutely zero athletic talent (and therefore zero athletic interest), so I felt like I had few ways to relate to other guys.

2. Growing up, my dad was affectionate but busy, while I shared an incredibly close relationship with my mom, so I was more apt to view women as safe places to share my feelings and struggles.

If you can relate, it should give you pause to consider these questions:

- **What do you feel are the defining characteristics of your own gender?** Specifically in reference to societal roles and expectations.

- **Is your view of your own gender generally positive or negative?** Why or why not?

- **How closely do you identify with your own gender?** Do you feel you have personal limitations which keep you from "measuring up" to your ideal of the perfect member of your gender? Why or why not?

These questions are not about "transgender" issues. I'm not trying to present gender as a social construct. However, beyond the created order, culture establishes gender norms and expectations, as does each person within every culture. And this interplay of creation and culture necessitates the following for healthy gender identity:

- Every man needs to hold a clear, healthy, and positive view of manhood and then be able to identify personally and positively with that view.

- Every woman needs to hold a clear, healthy, and positive view of womanhood and then be able to identify personally and positively with that view.

So, if you're the sort who seems to struggle with relating to (or even enjoying) your own gender, I would urge you to process the above questions with a couple of older, wiser mentor-types.

The Secret to Testing the Strength of Your Friendships

How do you know if you have same-gender friendships strong enough to support, guide, and cheer on a successful dating life?

The secret lies in answering this one question: do you have secrets your closest friends don't know? Be honest! Search your heart. Do you harbor any secrets—any at all—of which your closest same-gender friends have no knowledge?

- Abuse or trauma you've endured—especially physical or sexual
- Significant sin, deception, or offense on your part toward others
- Struggles with anxiety, depression, disorders, or addictions

Having close friends isn't all about "your dark side." These same-gender friends should know all the good there is to know about you and celebrate it with you!

- Personal hopes and aspirations
- Greatest accomplishments
- Favorite memories
- Character strengths
- Story of your spiritual growth

Don't have any secrets your closest friends don't already know? Great! Time for Prerequisite #4.

PREREQUISITE #4: YOU'RE COMFORTABLE RELATING TO THE OPPOSITE SEX

You would think feeling comfortable relating to the opposite sex would be a no-brainer when it came to knowing you were ready to date. After all, how could you hope to grow a friendship with someone that might lead to a life-giving, lifelong marriage when you don't even feel comfortable being around that someone?

Yet I have to specify this prerequisite because of two popular and powerful romantic myths sold by Hollywood.

Romantic Myth 1: When you meet the right person, relating to them will come easily.

You know the story line I'm talking about. Awkward, ugly duckling meets gorgeous swan who naturally awakens the hidden beauty and strength inside our little duckling. Who just so happens to turn out to be a swan too! Who knew?!

Why we believe it: Sometimes relationships just come together serendipitously (romances, friendships, artistic partnerships).

Why we should beware of it: Relationships with magical beginnings often don't last because magic doesn't sustain relationships. (People fall out of love, a new BFF becomes a former BFF, and bands break up.)

Romantic Myth 2: The right dating approach will make the right relationship work.

This story line usually requires help from friends who "know the code" like Buddy the Elf's step-brother, but bottom line, once you win their heart with the right setup, then you're in!

Why we believe it: Planning often pays off. As true in preparing for a date as it is a job interview.

Why we should beware of it: Healthy, authentic relationships are sustained by healthy, authentic individuals, not continual high-level strategy sessions.

In real life, if you don't feel comfortable relating to the opposite sex, then you don't feel comfortable relating to the opposite sex. Even the right person or the right setup (or both) won't overcome your lack of confidence and awkward nature in the long run.

Do You View the Opposite Sex in the Right Way?

Just as it is important to have a clear, accurate, and favorable view of your own gender, if we're going to relate to those of our opposing gender in the right way, we've got to view them in the right way.

But we often view members of the opposite sex as puzzles to solve, prizes to win, pawns to use, or perils to avoid.

The common thread in each of those perspectives? Viewing members of the opposite sex as objects we want to manipulate instead of people to whom we want to relate. And I'll admit, it's a challenge resisting the urge to view the opposite sex in these ways, even when you're married to one.

Does my wife, Julie, often seem like a conundrum wrapped in a mystery? Yes she does, but I have to resist the temptation to try to "solve" her like she's a problem. I must instead continually learn to relate to her in all her puzzling peculiarities.

Do I consider my wife a prize? Yes, but not a prize won from a carney trying to outwit me at the county fair but a prize received from God by His grace. She's not a trophy but a treasure.

Am I sometimes tempted to use Julie to get what I want? Yes, but healthy couples look for the win-win. No one should have to lose for the other to win.

Can my wife's priorities at times threaten my own? Yes again, but when I remember the enemy is never my wife, I can remember who the real threat is, the true enemy of my soul (and hers). Therefore, the true enemy of our marriage.

Now is the time to learn to recognize and counteract your own predisposition to view members of the opposite sex as objects you want to manipulate, and learn to approach them as people to whom you want to relate.

Stop Treating Dating like an Audition

We are prone to give more weight to the affirmation of the opposite sex than we should, like we're on *America's Got Talent*, and if one of those pretty people we've been trying so hard to impress hits the golden buzzer our future is set.

We don't usually obsess over how our same-gender friends view us. We're not looking for a golden buzzer from them. Subsequently, our lower expectations for same-gender relationships make it more likely our expectations will be met.

So do yourself a favor and stop auditioning for others, and simply seek to connect with them. Have a conversation. If you need a wingman or support team of friends to lower your stress level, there's no shame in that! But stop performing and start relating!

MATURITY IS KEY

Can you see how someone who's thriving in their close non-romantic relationships with family and friends, both dudes and dudettes, will have far greater success dating with rationality and not just emotionality.

Maturity really is key!

However, maturity simply isn't prized in our culture. In fact, it's worse than not being prized. Maturity is routinely mocked and even scorned. Consequently, few out there dating are mature enough to do so.

It's gotten so bad that many find heartbreak, rejection, and regret almost inescapable. And most will react to this fatalistic picture of dating in one of two ways:

1. Approach dating with a jaded attitude, seeking to get whatever they can in the moment (a free meal, a fun time, a hookup) without expecting to get what they really want long-term (genuine human connection, a significant other, marriage)

2. Avoid dating altogether out of fear, striving to keep all opposite-gender relationships "just friends," while attempting to suppress their sexual desires completely or while getting their "sexual needs" met through hooking up or porn

All along, the real problem is a simple (yet pronounced) lack of maturity because we are never taught how to be grown up.

Oh, the lost art of maturity. That's where we can take the reins of our lives and determine to become the person we were made to become! Are you ready to become that person?

YOU ARE MORE THAN A SEXUAL BEING

We go through sex ed in middle school (or elementary school, kindergarten, or whenever they're doing sex ed now), and there they unveil to us the mysteries of puberty. We learn how to cope with all the exciting changes that will be happening to our bodies (shower, apply deodorant, repeat), but we're not taught how to cope with the passions that result from the neurochemistry blowing up in our brains.

We learn the conditions necessary for our species to reproduce. We learn how successful conception can happen in a moment (so use a condom). But we are not taught the conditions necessary to raise the product of conception to full maturity.

Essentially, we're taught to be sexual beings, instead of social beings. Which is another way of saying we're taught to be more like animals than like humans. All the while, we are so much more than sexual or social; we are essentially spiritual beings, image-bearers of our Creator.

CHAPTER 17:

HOW TO KNOW GOD'S WILL FOR YOUR DATING LIFE

Every one of the six prerequisites for Romance 101 are all markers of relational maturity, but the last two are also markers of spiritual maturity, because if you are a follower of Christ, then that's the number one relationship in your life. And as you grow closer to Him, you naturally grow in the knowledge of God's will.

So if you want God's will for your dating life, this is your chapter.

PREREQUISITE #5: YOU ARE COMMITTED TO A STRONG CHRISTIAN COMMUNITY

Nothing concerns me more than when I meet someone who is desperately searching for somebody to give their heart to but is not the least bit concerned with investing their heart in a local body of believers.

And I meet a lot of "someones" like this.

- **Church-hoppers** who attend services weekly but change which congregation they attend every year or so (or month or so)

- **Church-shoppers** who regularly attend various student or young adult activities in their area but with no intention to commit to any one body

- **Church-samplers** who only attend services or events when they "feel the need"

However, if you aren't interested in committing to a Christian community, how can you know you're ready to commit to an individual in an exclusive dating relationship? Which commitment sounds like it would require more maturity?

In contrast, when I meet a young adult who is plugged into a community of believers where they are an intentional and active participant, I know that's a single person who's preparing to become a healthy, vibrant member of a healthy, vibrant couple. Is that you?

Regardless of your perspective, all of us are called to engage with—both receiving from and ministering to—a Christian community. All of us.

> *And let us consider how to stir up one another to love and good works, not neglecting to meet together, as is the habit of some, but encouraging one another, and all the more as you see the Day drawing near.* —Hebrews 10:24-25 ESV

The Church Needs You like You Need the Church

There's a difference in the unique socialization that takes place in a church that can't be compared to what you can find in other social arenas. A uniqueness that makes it essential for our spiritual growth and overall well-being.

> *For just as the body is one and has many members, and all the members of the body, though many, are one body, so it is with Christ.* —1 Corinthians 12:12 ESV

Unlike other groups, the members of a church are like members of a body. This isn't merely a way of saying we're each unique. It's specifically making the following two assertions:

1. Each member of a church is dependent on the other members of the body. (You need the church body.)

2. Each member of a church is an indispensable part of the body. (The church body needs you.)

Consider these words of Paul, later in 1 Corinthians 12:

> *But as it is, God arranged the members in the body, each one of them, as he chose. If all were a single member, where would the body be? As it is, there are many parts, yet one body. The eye cannot say to the hand, "I have no need of you," nor again the head to the feet, "I have no need of you."* —1 Cor 12:18-21 ESV

Paul declares we are dependent on each other to live this Christian life, so no believer should live as though they have no need of church commitment. Yet this is precisely how a believer is acting when they refuse to join themselves with a body of believers; like they've got it all going on, all on their own.

If we're going to believe scripture over our limited perspective, we must accept that believers need each other, that apart from a body we aren't merely incomplete, we are quite useless! As useless as an eye removed from the head or a head removed from the neck.

However, if we all need the body, then it logically follows that each of us is needed by the body. And Paul makes that clear later in 1 Corinthians 12:

> *On the contrary, the parts of the body that seem to be weaker are indispensable, and on those parts of the body that we think less honorable we bestow the greater honor, and our unpresentable parts are treated with greater modesty, which our more presentable*

206

> *parts do not require. But God has so composed the body, giving greater honor to the part that lacked it, that there may be no division in the body, but that the members may have the same care for one another. If one member suffers, all suffer together; if one member is honored, all rejoice together. Now you are the body of Christ and individually members of it.* —1 Cor 12:22-27 ESV

Every part of the body is indispensable. Necessary. Needed!

So while you need the church (whether you feel it or not), the church also needs you (whether you believe it or not). That said, even if you really can't see "what you get out of church," it's not all about you anyway. God did make the church for the good of every believer, but not for our enjoyment but His glory.

> *For by the grace given to me I say to everyone among you not to think of himself more highly than he ought to think, but to think with sober judgment, each according to the measure of faith that God has assigned. For as in one body we have many members, and the members do not all have the same function, so we, though many, are one body in Christ, and individually members one of another.* —Rom 12:3-5 ESV

So, I urge you, wise individual: stop resisting the will of God when it comes to church, and find a church body you can submit to, serve in, and be discipled by before you look for a human body you can love, honor, and cherish.

The Church Hop Leads to the Spouse Swap

I can't pretend that what God is asking us to do in the church comes naturally. It may be the vision, the goal, but it's seldom the experienced reality. Despite the level of difficulty, I urge you to double-down on your efforts toward church commitment if you want to be in a life-giving, lifelong marriage someday. Because if you approach church with a consumer mindset, you are actually practicing the very perspective that leads lovebirds to leave their marriage.

Consider the completely normal reasons we may justify changing churches, and then compare them to the corresponding reasons many justify divorce.

- I leave my church because I feel disconnected …
  And I leave my spouse because I lost that lovin' feeling.

- I leave my church because they're disorganized …
  And I leave my spouse because they're irresponsible.

- I leave my church because of personnel changes …
  And I leave my spouse because their personality changes.

- I leave my church because of a scandal …
  And I leave my spouse because of infidelity.

- I leave my church over hurt feelings …
  And I leave my spouse over irreconcilable differences.

- I leave my church because of unmet needs …
  And I leave my spouse for the exact same reason.

Commitment Doesn't Come Naturally

Believe it or not, there was never a time in history void of FOMO. We didn't use that acronym back then, but it's a force that's been real ever since the garden.

> *So when the woman saw that the tree was good for food, and that it was a delight to the eyes, and that the tree was to be desired to make one wise, she took of its fruit and ate, and she also gave some to her husband who was with her, and he ate.* —Genesis 3:6 ESV

Instead of holding fast to their commitment to God's command, they both succumbed to their flesh which didn't want to miss out on something "better."

So let's face it: commitment does indeed guarantee we will miss out on many things, but commitment to the right things ensures we will never miss out on the *best* things. This is the way God designed the world, with temptation built in, so we would have to choose time and time again to commit or to compromise.

The fact is, commitment will never come naturally. Because from the moment we realize our parents aren't the perfect caretakers we may have believed them to be, we learn people will let us down. So it's up to us to get our own needs met.

However, we were *designed* to need others, which means many of our needs can never be fully met outside of Christian community. So commitment is a requirement in life.

Commitment is also a learned skill, and the body of Christ offers a unique opportunity to learn how to do it! So man-up (or woman-up) and learn how to commit faithfully and serve sacrificially in an imperfect, but healthy, church body, and set yourself up for success in dating and eventually marriage!

Healthy Relationships Grow in Healthy Community

By the way, do you know who needs the church just as much as a single person?

A married person. Because healthy relationships don't grow in isolation. They grow in community.

Yes, sometimes in marriage it will be the two of you against the world, but that should not be the norm. Instead, in the long run, even the healthiest marriages survive only because they are invested in a church body that needs healthy families as much as healthy families need the church.

PREREQUISITE #6: GOD IS FIRST IN YOUR LIFE

Now we come down to our last prerequisite for Romance 101, and it's the key. God needs to be first in your life! Not in your Top 10, Top 5, or even tied for first, but el numero uno.

Why? Because nothing will test whether God is truly first in your life like a serious dating relationship. Even some of the most faithful disciples of Jesus will be tempted to drop Jesus down to the #2 position when madly in love with someone. Even when that someone is a fellow believer who loves Jesus too.

Before you test your love for God by pursuing a serious crush, make sure you prepare for that test like you want to crush it. In fact, I urge you to pause and pray right now, asking God's Holy Spirit to help you discern if God is truly first in your life, even as you're reading these words.

I'm serious! Right now.

A Prayer to Put God First

Did you do it? Did you pray?

If not, at least consider praying this prayer:

> Heavenly Father,
>
> I truly do want You to be first in my life in everything! I want to worship You and You alone. I want to abide in Your love in every waking moment. I want to treasure Your truth and wisdom. I want to cherish this life as a gift from You and a gift to You. And I want Your love to fill me and flow out of me into the lives of others. Even those I date. *Especially* those I date!

I want this because I want to date with total faith in Your sovereignty, certainty of Your goodness, agreement with Your word, submission to Your commands, and passion for Your glory.

So please, O Holy Spirit, please search my heart, mind, soul, body, and every relationship, and reveal any and every area of compromise. That I not only would stand faithful to You, but inspire and lead others to love and trust You in all things. Even those I date. *Especially those I date!*

In Jesus name, I pray. Amen!

What Could Possibly Shock Angels?

Of course, God Himself is never shocked or surprised by anything, but check out these words He proclaims through the prophet Jeremiah:

> *Be appalled, O heavens, at this; be shocked, be utterly desolate, declares the Lord.* —Jeremiah 2:12 ESV

The Hebrew word for "be shocked" is also interpreted in the NASB as "be horribly afraid," and the Hebrew word translated as "be utterly desolate" lends the idea of being laid waste or completely destroyed or devastated.

What in the world would the God of the universe want the heavens, His throne room, to be so upset about? We continue reading in verse 12:

> *For my people have committed two evils.* —Jeremiah 2:13a ESV

Two evils! Well of course evil should be shocking! But what two evils could they be?! Sexual immorality and murder? Abortion and pollution? Terrorism and human trafficking?

Be appalled, O heavens, at this; be shocked, be utterly desolate,
declares the Lord, for my people have committed two evils: they
have forsaken me, the fountain of living waters, and hewed out
cisterns for themselves, broken cisterns that can hold no water.
—Jeremiah 2:12-13 ESV

What did the word of the LORD, through Jeremiah, identify as the two appalling, horrifying, and devastating crimes of the house of Jacob?

1. They have forsaken me, the fountain of living waters
2. They have hewed out cisterns for themselves,
   broken cisterns that can hold no water

If those accusations seem pretty benign to you compared to sex trafficking or murder, you wouldn't be alone in thinking so. That's exactly the way Jeremiah's audience received his words. With a collective yawn. "Really? That's it?"

Yes! Really! That's it! Because what's being described here is not a preference in where to find liquid but where to find *life*. It's not about water. It's about worship!

Let's not forget that in Jeremiah's day, they didn't get to choose between bottled, filtered, tap, sparkling, iced, or room-temp. Back then water was something you had to look for and something you needed to store up.

Even still, we all know we'd die without clean water, and that's why God uses the search for water to express who He is. He is the one and only source of life! TRUE LIFE! The fountain of living waters. The *only* fountain of living waters, by the way! The living water we were made to drink of deeply and often.

O God, you are my God; earnestly I seek you; my soul thirsts for
you; my flesh faints for you, as in a dry and weary land where
there is no water. So I have looked upon you in the sanctuary,

beholding your power and glory. Because your steadfast love is
better than life, my lips will praise you. —Psalm 63:1-3 ESV

Then, what's the next horror? That instead of coming to Him for everything we need, we will go to great lengths to meet our own needs. We'll look to money and therefore our career and therefore our education. We'll look to security and therefore legislation and therefore our government. And we'll look to romantic love and therefore a significant other and therefore our dating life.

To help us understand these two sins, consider the question God poses through Jeremiah in the previous verse:

Has a nation changed its gods, even though they are no gods? But
my people have changed their glory for that which does not profit.
—Jeremiah 2:11 ESV

So we discover that idolatry is the root of the whole problem.

And when it comes to dating, you have probably seen (or at least heard) there is almost nothing else more likely to become an idol than a crush, which becomes a romance, which becomes an obsession.

There's just something about romantic love that seems so much more wonderful than God's love. And God finds that appalling, horrifying, and devastating.

But we must understand this perspective is not born out of personal offense, like we're hurting God's feelings. God's concern is not for *His* good, but *ours*.

Why God Cares So Much About Idolatry

What's the big deal with idolatry? Is God some cosmic narcissist or what? Is His ego really so delicate that He can't share a little affection?

For the answer, let's clarify the two evils from Jeremiah 2:

1. They have forsaken me, the fountain of living waters
2. They have hewed out cisterns for themselves,
   broken cisterns that can hold no water

Who's missing out on anything in this passage? God? God does claim to be forsaken, but who does He claim to *be*? Is He the fountain *in need* of living water? No! He is the fountain *of* living water!

Who needs the living water?

We do! We are the ones in need of living water, not God. And what do we do with our desperate need? We try to meet it ourselves. Like we can do it on our own. Like we can do it better.

Does this hurt God's feelings? Does He "need to feel needed" or something? Hardly. It is He who is the ultimate need-meeter. As Jesus stated to the Samaritan woman by the well:

> *"If you knew the gift of God, and who it is that is saying to you,*
> *'Give me a drink,' you would have asked him, and he would have*
> *given you living water."* —John 4:10 ESV

Then why all the angst?! If God is as self-sufficient and omniscient and omnipotent as He claims, why does He call heaven to desolation, all because we want to try to take care of ourselves? Is He a drama queen? I mean, drama king?

No! He is the King of kings! And not only that, He is our faithful Father who scans the horizon for the return of His wayward son. He is the Wonderful Counselor who holds the healing power of wisdom. He is the good Teacher who knows the truth which will set us free! He is the gracious Master who gives us the very work we were born to do. And He is the precious Friend, who simply loves our presence and delights to offer us His own presence.

As Jesus continued in His conversation with the woman by the well:

> *"Everyone who drinks of this water will be thirsty again, but whoever drinks of the water that I will give him will never be thirsty again. The water that I will give him will become in him a spring of water welling up to eternal life."* —John 4:13-14 ESV

So, God is not calling heaven to despair over how disappointing we've all proven to be to Him, but how brokenhearted He is for us. He needs us not in the least, but He loves us beyond imagining. And He is for us!

Do you feel your need for Him?

And beyond *feeling* your need, have you learned to trust Him to meet your every need? Until you do, you will keep digging well after well after well, hoping to meet your own needs, hoping to feel alive.

The last thing you need is to make your dating life one of those many broken wells which drain life out of you instead of bringing life to you.

HOW ARE YOUR PREREQUISITES?

None of the six prerequisites for Romance 101 are as fun as catching the eye of a beautiful creature across the room, flirting with and teasing the people you're interested in, or being in a relationship with someone who thinks you hung the moon.

They aren't as fun as all that, but they are all more real—more meaningful. And these relational objectives will form a foundation for guiding your dating life and supporting your growing relationship when the time is right.

ARE YOU READY TO GROW THAT FRIENDSHIP?

To remind you, we shared these six prerequisites to help you gauge your maturity level so you could know if you are truly ready to grow the kind of friendship that might lead to a life-giving, lifelong marriage.

Next up? Some guidelines in actually growing that kind of friendship once you've determined you are ready to date.

This chapter marks the end of the sixth lesson in an 8-week LoveEd study. For discussion questions and resources go to:

FMUniversity.net/DatePrep-wk6

CHAPTER 18:

DEFINE THE PERSON BEFORE YOU DEFINE THE RELATIONSHIP

When you have romantic feelings for someone, it's normal to want to declare them to your beloved. It's also normal to fear doing so until you confirm the person you like likes you back.

Even if you're not necessarily crushing on someone, but you've been hanging out with them for some time, it's natural to wonder: *What is this relationship we're in together? Is it just a friendship? Is it more? Do I want it to be more? Could it be more? Should it be more?*

When Julie and I were in college, they called it the DTR talk. The talk where you Define The Relationship. And in many ways, in the good old-fashioned conservative dating world, where hooking up is still considered wrong, this is more or less the goal of dating: discovering if you share mutual feelings of romantic interest or if one of you is about to get friend-zoned.

DON'T FEAR THE FRIEND-ZONE

Getting friend-zoned is no fun. I can attest to this. Multiple times. And it happened to me when I wasn't even trying to build a friendship first. I was looking for mutual attraction right away!

That said, the pain of all those rejections couldn't compare to the kind of heartbreak you endure when a romantic relationship, where both of you are totally into each other, nevertheless dies.

This is why we recommend that before you have the Define the Relationship talk, where you seek to confirm mutual physical attraction, you first have at least ten DTP talks.

Those would be Define the Person talks, where you endeavor to learn whether the two of you could actually become good friends. The kind of friends who could not only put up with each other for the rest of your lives but actually enjoy it.

YOU CAN'T RUSH THE PROCESS

Though I'm calling them DTP talks, to play off the idea of a DTR talk, please understand I am not actually suggesting you cover all ten topics of conversation over the course of ten talks, or even ten dates. Instead, here are your objectives:

1. Make sure you at least address all of these subjects before you ever consider dating seriously.

2. Make sure you thoroughly cover these topics before you consider engagement.

We'll begin with the DTP talks you need to start having before the first date. In fact, you can have this first DTP talk before you even *meet* the person you're interested in because this conversation shouldn't even be with them but with those who know them well.

DTP TALK #1: REPUTATION

We acquire reputations for a reason: we build them, one choice at a time.

This is important to remember when you're dating with the goal of marriage, because if you marry someone you will have to live with their choices for the rest of your life. So, you need to know the reputation of the person you're dating.

For starters, you want to make sure they don't already have a reputation for being any of the nine Mr. or Ms. Wrongs we discussed in Chapters 4–6. Beyond asking: watch, pay attention, and observe the person—not in a stalker kind of way—but in a prudent kind of way. As you do, consider any of the following questions:

- Do they demonstrate a passion for Christ in their speech and behavior?

- Are they known for spiritual courage or compromise?

- Can they hold their tongue?

- Are they more likely to be self-deprecating, self-promoting, or not thinking of themselves at all?

- Emotionally, do they come across timid, careful, wise, courageous, carefree, or reckless?

- Intellectually, do they come across illiterate, naïve, well-informed, persuasive, opinionated, or obstinate?

- Do they demonstrate a growth mindset that enjoys learning and experiencing new things?

- When it comes to stewarding their possessions, do they tend to be careless, sloppy, clean, meticulous, or OCD?

- Do they take good care of their bodies through diet and exercise?

- Are they tightfisted, thrifty, generous, or wasteful with their money?

- What's the reputation of their friends and associates?

- In their social circles, do they tend to control, lead, follow, or challenge?

- Are they more well-loved, respected, appreciated, tolerated, or avoided?

- Are they dependable or flaky?

- How do they respond to correction? Do they reject it, take offense to it, ignore it, appreciate it, or act on it?

- Will they confront someone in the wrong? And if so, do they do so fearfully, confidently, graciously, abruptly, or arrogantly?

- With conflict, do they tend to escalate it, enjoy it, address it, tolerate it, avoid it, or fear it?

- With offenses, do they tend to stuff their feelings, forgive, or hold grudges?

- What is their dating history and is it readily known by those who know them?

- Is their approach to dating more impulsive, flippant, casual, intentional, anxious, overbearing, or desperate?

- Do they date around a lot?

- Do they tend to rush into serious relationships?

- Are they known for leading people on or leaving people hanging?

- Do they jump from serious relationship to serious relationship?

For that matter, how would you answer the previous questions for yourself?

Online Versus in Real Life

While we're on the subject of reputation, we can't overlook someone's online profile, so carefully consider where and how they present themselves online.

Of course, our online image often differs from who we are In Real Life (IRL). Moreover, we will often present ourselves differently even between online platforms (one's online dating profile could be very different from their Twitter posts which could be very different from their Instagram stories).

Some of this can be explained by the differences between the platforms. However, there's often more behind this reality, so here are just two contrasting tendencies to watch out for when stalking someone (in a Christ-like way) online:

1. **Idealization:** Their online profile may be more idealized because they want to present a version of themself that either they believe others will like more or they wish they were. Or both.

2. **Impropriety:** Their online behavior may be more vulnerable, imprudent, abrasive, or even crude since they are able to "hide behind a screen."

That said, if you notice a symmetry between the way someone presents themselves online and IRL or even a constancy between someone's various online profiles, that is compelling evidence of a person secure in who they are and who they are striving to become.

A True (and Very Sad) Story

"I've never seen him like this before!"

"He's changed so much since he met you!"

"He's like a totally different person now!"

Those words from Barry's (not his real name) family and friends made Sandy (nor her real name) feel so good, so special. As if the way Barry treated her didn't make her feel special enough.

Those sweet words were also the only warning she had that her future marriage would turn out to be a fantastic disaster.

Frankly, it wasn't bad being the person responsible for changing a man for the better. She seemed like a superhero amongst his family and friends. (And it's important for family and friends to support your relationship, right?)

But after Barry and Sandy said, "I do," in front of all those approving well-wishers, Sandy discovered Barry wasn't done changing.

Only now he changed back to the flaming narcissist he had been known as prior to meeting Sandy.

Even worse—devastatingly so—Barry quickly made it clear he had married Sandy only for her money. He didn't even want to have sex with her. (He had porn to take care of those urges.)

The moral of this relational horror story: reputation matters.

What About Second Chances?

Can people change? Certainly. Can they experience dramatic change? Absolutely!

Every day, star-crossed lovers change dramatically. Formerly depressed, lonely, broken, and empty, the power of romance turns their frowns upside down, heals every hurt in their hearts, and fills their lives with love and meaning.

Of course, people change for other reasons, more significant and lasting than infatuation, but the sad reality is that many dramatic changes aren't permanent ones. Think about someone who suddenly loses a lot of weight or comes into a lot of money.

Remember, people garner reputations for a reason, so if you find yourself in Sandy's position in the previous story, STOP.

First, dig in deep to discover precisely who your love interest used to be and what has brought about such significant transformation. If the change is sincere, they should be very open about recounting who they once were and delight in sharing the details of their transformation. In contrast, watch out for both of these extremes:

- Shame—Are they embarrassed to admit their past sins? Do they appear to be free of that guilt, or do they still seem bound by it?

- Pride—Does their confession sound more like bragging? Do they take full responsibility for their past or do they try to whitewash or excuse certain behaviors?

Don't just take their word for it. Consult those who know them best. Then, if you discover you're the apparent catalyst for their life change? RUN!

If someone has changed overnight in a permanent way, it can only be the result of a profound life experience. As much as we'd all like to be the "profound life experience" of someone else, odds are we won't be.

If the change is genuine, it will be proven over time. So give it time. Indeed, if your beloved has truly changed, they shouldn't be offended that you want to take a year or more to make sure. No rush. Remember love is first and foremost patient. Oh yeah, and remember, reputation matters.

That said, reputations are not always reputable. That's why you need to advance to DTP Talk #2.

DTP TALK #2: CHARACTER

Reputation is who others *think* you are, but character is who you *really* are. While you might date someone for their reputation, if you end up married to them, you will have to live with their character. Every day. Until one of you dies.

In a perfect world, someone's reputation would naturally flow out of their character. However, in the real world, someone projecting a sterling reputation could be hiding secrets which suggest a character that's anything but sterling.

Sadly, this possibility is even more likely inside the church community where bad behavior is less tolerated. This means you may not get any warning from friends and family saying things such as, "They've changed so much since they met you!" Therefore, you must be willing to take the time and do the hard work necessary to discern the true character of the person you're dating.

How to Determine Someone's True Character

The saying goes, "character is who you are when no one's watching." But how are you supposed to find out who someone is "when no one's watching" while you're watching them?

Honest answer? You can't.

But don't let that discourage you! Let that inspire you to do two things:

1. Take. Your. Time!
2. Pay. Attention!

Sad truth: most people date with their eyes half closed and then when they get married and the power of limerence fades, their eyes are opened, and they see the character issues they ignored when they were dating. (And that's another reason why we have divorce.)

So, in honor of dating with your eyes wide open, here are a plethora of questions for you to address over time.

Relational Questions:

- How do they treat people in authority?
  Do they resent them or respect them?

- How do they treat people who are serving them or work for them?
  Do they disparage them or treat them with dignity?

- Do they talk about people behind their backs?
  In front of their backs?

- How do they talk about their past loves?
  Was everything their ex's fault?

- How do they talk about their family, especially their parents (or the people who raised them)? Do they tend to idolize, admire, or criticize them?

Emotional Questions:

- How well do they respond to disappointment?
  Do they sulk, rage, or whine?

- How do they respond to success? Do they brag? Slack off?

- What are their fears? Do they center around money, career, family, health, or zombies?

- How do they deal with their fears? Do they tend to worry about them, suppress them, or face them?

- From where do they seem to draw their strength: from within, from the approval and support of others, or from an authentic relationship with God? How can you tell?

Material Questions:

- Are they responsible with money? Carry debt thoughtlessly? Spend frivolously? Give generously? Save frugally?

- Are they responsible with time? Plan? Flexible? Waste it with hours of entertainment? Invest it in reading and watching FMU material?

- Are they responsible with possessions? Are they obsessive or careless? Do they hoard or do they share?

- In all these areas do they tend to act more like stewards, owners, or renters?

Integrity Questions:

- How open are they about admitting their "rough spots"? Do they appear more defensive, humbly honest, or blissfully unaware?

- How do they deal with their character deficiencies? Do they seem more passive, apologetic, or intentional about taking steps to change?

- Do they learn from their mistakes and subsequently break recurring patterns of failure, or do they just seem to repeat them?

- Can they share a past struggle where they have found victory or at least measurable and sustainable progress?

I know that's a lot of ground to cover, and most people don't learn the answers to most of these questions until after marriage. And that's another reason we have divorce. But that won't be your story.

Of course, if all the above questions were on a test, most of us (perhaps all of us) would flunk, but that shouldn't mean you just throw caution to the wind, close your eyes, and kiss. That's how our culture wound up in this mess.

DTP TALK #3: INTERESTS

Now for the fun stuff. Find out what the person you're dating is interested in. And just as importantly, what they aren't interested in.

- Career, work, and education
- Food: cooking, baking, and eating
- Movies, shows, recreation, and sports
- Art, music, and poetry
- Health and fitness
- Faith, theology, and church
- Travel, hobbies, and fashion
- Books, podcasts, blogs, and vlogs

As you discover what your date is interested in, here are some questions you can use to learn more about your date:

- How did you come to be involved in [insert interest here]?

- With whom have you most often shared [insert interest here]?

- What are some fun/meaningful/favorite memories of enjoying [insert interest here]?

- What challenges have you overcome as you have pursued [insert interest here]?

- What future aspirations do you have for [insert interest here]?

Beware of Focusing on Common Interests

Like in any relationship, you will naturally gravitate toward interests you share with your date, and for the first date or two, that is an effective and comfortable way of getting to know someone.

However, there is a danger in keeping your conversation centered on common interests. Here are six in particular:

1. You keep the conversation more self-focused, as you only talk about the interests you share with your date.

2. You keep yourself from learning new things.

3. You miss the chance to see how open your date is to learning new things themselves (or how self-focused they may be).

4. You can acquire an inaccurate picture of your date if one or more of their greatest interests differ from your shared interests.

5. You can project an inaccurate picture of yourself if one or more of your own greatest interests differ from your shared interests.

6. You can both be misled to believe you're more compatible than you really are because you never explore your differences.

In short, focusing on common interests is good for getting to know someone as an acquaintance or even as a casual friend (which is what you are doing in the earliest stages of a dating relationship), but it is an inadequate way of getting to know someone as a potential life partner.

The Goal Is Not to Make the Relationship Work

If you see the purpose of dating as growing a friendship that might lead to a life-giving, lifelong marriage, then you need to find out if your relationship can really work long-term.

But what many are tempted to do is work hard to *make* the relationship work. Working to *make* a relationship work is different from seeking to find out if it *can* work.

I'm not saying it doesn't take work to make a relationship ... ah ... work. It always does, because intimate relationships require personal growth, selflessness, compromise, communication, repentance, forgiveness, and a bunch of other things which require work.

However, many a desperate dater will bend over backward to do what their partner wants, converse about what their partner cares about, and even be who their partner wants them to be. Until they get married.

Then they just want to be themselves. This is a recipe for disappointment at best, disaster at worst. So why not discover early on if you really enjoy being around each other. This means two things:

1. Let go of the insecurity that comes from wanting to be liked, accepted, and approved, and find out if your date will like, accept, and approve of you even if they don't share your interests.

2. Let go of the need for the relationship to work out, and find out if you can genuinely enjoy the person you're dating, even if you don't share their interests.

More than simply enjoying each other in spite of your inevitable differences, discover if you can actually *enjoy* your differences. In a healthy relationship, differences can make each of you more interesting, as it broadens each of your horizons.

DTP TALK #4: IDENTITY

As you get to know your date, you want to move from discussing *common* interests to discovering their *core* interests.

Is the person you're dating someone who watches sports or someone who lives and breathes sports? Do they enjoy their career or are they married to their career? Do they go to church or are they committed to their church? Do they know Jesus or do they adore and delight in Him?

To aid you in this mission, here are some questions to consider asking your date:

- What interests could they never imagine changing?

- Would they rather engage in [insert interest here] or [insert interest here]?

- What significant sacrifices have they given up for [insert interest here]?

- What would they be willing to sacrifice to realize their future dream for [insert interest here]?

- Have they seen ways [insert interest here] has changed them? For better? For worse?

- How do they feel about themselves when they've had a successful experience with [insert interest here]?

- What about when they've had a bad experience with [insert interest here]? How have they worked through that?

- How do their friends and family feel about their passion for [insert interest here]?

Bottom line: you want to discern your date's core interests because they will be guideposts to discovering where they derive their identity.

Beware of Identity Theft

You want to date someone whose identity is securely rooted because if it's not, your lover is going to be looking to you to tell them who they are.

Sadly, with the decline of the family in our culture today, there are many out there who will want you to tell them who they are. They hope to discover who they are through dating: to have their dating life validate them, give them meaning, and prove their worth.

Of course, until we're dead, we're always growing in the knowledge of who we are, but when you realize the person you're dating is more or less willing to be whoever you want them to be, that is a red flag. A. Bright. Red. Flag. We call this identity theft. (That said, make sure *you* know who *you* are before you date, lest you be the one perpetrating identity theft.)

Now admittedly, being the source of someone else's identity is pretty fun at first. It certainly can make you feel awfully special, but it grows tiring, stressful, and suffocating fairly quickly. Then you're left feeling more awful than awfully special.

So beware of identity theft. You want to *discern* the identity of your love interest, not *give* them their identity.

CHAPTER 19:

WHY YOU DON'T HAVE TIME TO MAKE OUT ON A DATE

It takes a significant investment of time to truly grow a friendship. And if you hope that friendship might lead to a life-giving, lifelong marriage? Well, you ought to expect to put in your time.

Yet, like anything else in life, your Time Spent Dating (TSD) is limited, so limited, you want to maximize your Time Spent Growing a Friendship (TSGF) on every date, but several things will compete with that.

- Time Spent Flirting (TSF)
- Time Spent in Small Talk (TSST)
- Time Spent Watching Entertainment (TSWE)
- Time Spent on Your Phone (TSYP)
- Time Spent Making Out (TSMO)

The flirting can waste a good portion of the first couple of dates, and the time spent in small talk, watching entertainment, and on your phone can be significant time sucks on *any* relationship. However, when it comes to a romantic relationship, it's the Time Spent Making Out that can quickly grow to monopolize all your TSD, leaving little time left over to grow a friendship.

That's why the point of outlining these ten Define The Person Talks is not merely to discourage you from making out but to open your eyes to the fact that you don't really have time to make out in the first place. Even though in our culture, TSMO is generally perceived as one of the best parts of dating. Maybe even the main point.

You simply can't spend excessive time making out *and* spend sufficient time getting to know your date. It's not entirely either/or, but pretty close. So you need to be brutally honest with yourself. Do you truly want to get to know your date or just get frisky?

WHICH COUPLE WOULD YOU WANT TO BE?

To help us see the impact of the tradeoff between relational intimacy and physical intimacy, let's look at how two different couples invest/spend their TSD over the course of 90 days. In Chapter 14 we talked about the opportunity cost of making out. In comparing these two couple's profiles, we'll flesh that out.

Couple 1: The Frisky Kittens

Time Spent Dating: 104 hours

They went out on a total of 26 dates (about two a week) spending four hours on average per date. Dates in the first month were under two hours, but, due to the couples TSMO (or more honestly TSHS: Time Spent Having Sex), dates lasted far longer toward the third month. (Indeed, four dates turned into "sleepovers.")

Time Spent Making Out: 52 hours

They spent far less time making out in the first month, but by the last month, making out (or hooking up, or just plain ol' sex) was pretty much all they wanted to do. And all they were doing.

DATE LIKE YOU KNOW WHAT YOU'RE DOING

Time Spent Growing a Friendship: 13 hours

On average, they invested 30 minutes each date in getting to know each other, but most of that time was invested in the first few dates, before sexual intimacy took over their dating life.

After all the TSMO, along with small talk, entertainment, and phone distraction, there simply wasn't much time to grow a friendship. And honestly, once the sleepovers started, they could have cared less about a friendship or marriage, as making out was so fun and exhilarating and made them feel far closer than best friends.

Couple 2: The Conscientious Cats

Time Spent Dating: 52 hours

They went out on a total of 13 dates (just one a week) and only spent about two hours on average per date. Like the first couple, dates lasted longer the longer they dated, but unlike the first couple, this was *not* due to their TSMO.

Time Spent Making Out: 0 hours

They kept their dating life out in the open where they wouldn't be tempted to do any "speaking in tongues" or "laying on of hands." But it was clear after only a month that their physical attraction was mutual, even though they didn't focus on that aspect of their relationship.

Time Spent Growing a Friendship: 19.5 hours

Of course, they spent some time in small talk at the beginning and end of every date, and they also watched a couple of movies together, but they established a "No Phone" rule for official dates, allowing them to invest the vast majority of that time in intentional conversations. Enough time to know they were both interested in continuing to get to know each other better and that there was more they *needed* to get to know.

That said, during those 90 days they also spent many hours together in non-date group gatherings with friends from church and work where they were able to see more of each other's character and friends instead of more of each other's bodies. So their actual TSGF was much higher than just 19.5 hours.

ONLY ONE OF THESE DATING PATTERNS WILL WORK

By analyzing these two radically different approaches to dating, we can make the following observations:

- Over the course of three months, the Frisky Kittens spent twice as much time together on dates as the Conscientious Cats did.

- The extra time the Frisky Kittens spent together made them feel far closer to each other than the Conscientious Cats felt at the end of those 90 days, especially since the Friskies were spending so much time in physical intimacy, even having sex and sleeping over.

- In spite of spending only half the time together on dates, the Conscientious Cats wound up investing 50% more of that time actually getting to know each other. When you add in the small group activities, our Conscientious couple probably invested twice as much time growing a friendship.

- The extra time the Conscientious Cats invested in getting to know each other enabled them to grow a far more meaningful friendship in 90 days, even though they didn't necessarily feel as close as the Friskies felt.

In short: after 90 days, the Friskies knew far less about each other, and yet felt far closer than the Conscientious, setting their respective relationships on two very different trajectories.

Indeed, in spite of truly enjoying their time together and growing both in friendship and respect for each other, in those three short months, our Conscientious couple discovered a couple issues which would keep their relationship from moving forward if they couldn't work through them. That's why on their next date they'll be meeting up with a married couple they both respect who they hope can give them some wise counsel.

Meanwhile, after 90 days, the only thing our Frisky Kittens really know about each other is that they really enjoy having sex. They haven't even begun having the kind of conversations which would allow them to discover the sort of issues the Conscientious Cats are concerned with.

Not that the Friskies were always happy together. In fact, they had two serious yelling matches in their third month (they called them lover's quarrels). But they made up and made out after each and then slept on it (together) both times. In spite of all this, their next date is a weekend getaway, and if that goes well, they plan on moving in together.

Here's the disturbing reality: the dating pattern of the Frisky Kittens is considered perfectly normal today while the dating pattern of the Conscientious Cats is almost unheard of.

Yet, I hope when you look at their stories, you can see how easily following the Frisky pattern almost inevitably leads to heartbreak, rejection, and regret. But in the meantime, this dating pattern will easily have them sharing rent and utilities in less than six months.

By the time their relationship implodes and one of them moves out, their lives will be so intertwined they will feel like they're getting a divorce, even though they were never married. Can you see how choosing to pursue relational intimacy over physical intimacy dramatically impacts a dating relationship?

If so, then you'll see the importance of having these next three DTP talks.

DTP TALK #5: VALUES

Sharing personal interests on a date requires a fraction of the vulnerability required when sharing personal values. That's one of the reasons we are tempted to keep our dating conversations from moving beyond discussing and comparing interests.

However, which is more *important* to discover: your date's interests or values?

Of course, the answer is obvious. If you don't have a firm grasp of the values of the person you're dating, you can't have any idea about the wisdom of committing to them in an exclusive dating relationship.

But that's why it's so important to wade out from the shallow waters of interests into the deeper waters of values. Even early in a dating relationship.

Beware of Focusing on Shared Values

As with interests, remember the goal is to discover what your date values most (or not at all), and in turn, to honestly share what you value most (or not at all).

However, just like sharing interests, the temptation is to focus only on shared values and avoid discussing areas where you suspect, fear, or know your personal values will clash.

Actually, an even scarier temptation couples fall into is simply taking the values they want to discover in a significant other and presuming them or projecting them onto the person they're dating. And someone who's really into you (or who really wants to manipulate you) will often comply with this desire, reflecting back to you whatever values they perceive you want them to hold.

That's a nice way of saying that many will lie about their values, which is why you need to move to DTP Talk #6.

DTP TALK #6: CONVICTIONS

Truth is, many will never consider what someone's convictions are, as I describe them here. And many aren't even aware of what their *own* convictions are, thinking their values comprise all there is to talk about when it comes to their personal morality. Yet here are the important distinctions I make between the two:

- Your **values** are *important*,
  but your **convictions** are *imperative*.

- Your **values** will *describe* you,
  but your **convictions** will *define* you.

- Your **values** will generally *direct* your decisions,
  but your **convictions** will ultimately *determine* your decisions.

- You will *defend* your **values**,
  but you will *die* for your **convictions**.

For example, someone who holds sexual purity as a personal value, but not as a true conviction, might want to save sex for marriage but will frequently push the boundaries of physical touch from the friendly to the sexual.

While someone who values family, but has no real convictions about it, might want to put their family first, but in practice, meeting demands at work will override their commitments to family almost every time.

Hypocrite or Weakling?

Many of us espouse values which we believe in our heart of hearts are right. Yet when temptation hits, we fail to hold fast.

It makes me think of Jesus's disciples falling asleep in the garden as He cried out to His Father, sweating drops of blood. We know His disciples loved Him dearly, but they couldn't keep their eyes open and mouths praying.

> *Watch and pray that you may not enter into temptation. The spirit indeed is willing, but the flesh is weak.* —Matthew 26:41 & Mark 14:38 ESV

The spirit is willing, but the flesh is weak. Can you relate?

I can! I truly did value sexual purity in my dating life. I not only wanted to hold onto my virginity, I wanted to honor God with my body, and I wanted to honor the bodies of every girl I dated.

So I did. Until Julie. As I already confessed in Chapter 4, we made it to the marriage bed as virgins but not sexually pure.

Sexual purity was clearly not a conviction. It was important but not imperative. Therefore, it did *not* define our dating relationship. Instead, when tempted, desire determined my decisions. Not conviction. And, in the end, instead of dying for my convictions, I sacrificed them for the pleasure of the moment.

What I did not realize then is that when I sacrificed my convictions for the pleasure of the moment, I also forfeited peace I hoped to enjoy in the future. Remember, all that messing around prior to our wedding day messed with our sexual enjoyment for a good seven to ten years after our wedding day.

Convictions Call for Action

If you're violating something you claim is a conviction for you, then you need to do something about it, something more effective than just "trying harder."

If someone is convicted of a crime, there is a sentence that follows, and then authorities step in to enforce the conditions of that sentence.

But what happens when the Holy Spirit convicts you of sin? Do you just confess, until the next time, or do you take steps to ensure there won't be a next time? Have you submitted your life—particularly your dating life—to the accountability of older and wiser family, mentors, and friends? If you have true convictions you're failing to uphold, you will. Because convictions call for action.

Judge the Fruit, Not the Intentions

When discerning which of your date's values are truly convictions, the goal is not to judge the heart of the person you're dating. You can't really know their intentions. You only need to judge the fruit: the evidence of their maturity and character revealed by their words and actions. And if they don't line up with their professed values, you know those values aren't true convictions.

With this knowledge you can make a wiser, more well-informed decision about continuing, pausing, or ending your relationship. And I would urge you to seek the wise counsel of someone who knows you well and loves God well in making that decision. Because, in the end, upholding values is hard work. It's easier to settle for less, and so, over time, we only wind up sticking with our convictions.

That said, if you're going to spend the rest of your life with someone, don't you want to know which of their values they're going to die for and which they will sacrifice? Then you need to date in such a way as to find that out.

Know Your Own Convictions

There is a critical prerequisite to discerning the true convictions of others: knowing your own convictions first.

> *For with the judgment you pronounce you will be judged, and with the measure you use it will be measured to you. Why do you see the speck that is in your brother's eye, but do not notice the log that is in your own eye? Or how can you say to your brother, "Let me take the speck out of your eye," when there is the log in your own eye?*

You hypocrite, first take the log out of your own eye, and then you will see clearly to take the speck out of your brother's eye.
—Matthew 7:2-5 ESV

Not only is it hypocritical to judge the convictions of others before judging your own, in learning to discern your own convictions, you learn how to do the same with others.

Added bonus: you get to know yourself better. If you can't know the person you're dating without knowing their true convictions, how can you know yourself without knowing the same?

DTP TALK #7: COMPATIBILITY

As you're gathering the facts about your date, learning about their interests, identity, values, and convictions, it's only natural (and logical and wise) to consider how compatible your own interests, identity, values, and convictions are with the person you're dating.

In fact, in addition to the criterion we've already covered in our first four DTP talks, there are numerous dimensions in which you might want to be compatible with someone you would consider spending the rest of your life with. Here are just a few:

- Religious beliefs and traditions
- Exercise and dietary expectations, disciplines, and restrictions
- Career aspirations and priorities
- Financial priorities and perspective
- Communication patterns and expectations
- Social temperaments, preferences, and expectations
- Family background and traditions
- Marital roles and expectations
- Parenting aspirations, roles, and expectations

Again, even though we list all the above under the heading of one Define The Person *Talk*, please understand it should take you many talks over the course of many dates—perhaps many months—to cover all of the afore-mentioned topics both thoroughly, yet naturally.

Further clarification: the above isn't a checklist. It's not even comprehensive. It's merely meant to open your mind to the vast array of compatibilities (or incompatibilities) possible in a dating relationship.

The goal isn't to be "compatible" in every area. That's not going to happen. With *anyone.* However, wherever you aren't compatible in marriage you will have to make compromises or you will have to expect conflict.

When it comes to casual, noncommitted, or distant relationships you can just avoid areas of incompatibility, but a healthy marriage is neither casual, noncommitted, nor distant, so these are your only options when it comes to every area of possible compatibility:

- Compatible
- Compromise
- Conflict

What About Sexual Compatibility?

You might have noticed I was missing a compatibility discussed and debated about far more than any of the compatibilities listed previously. Namely sexual compatibility.

There's an important reason for that omission. Namely that after twenty-eight years of monogamous sexual experience, I am strongly convinced that sexual compatibility is a red herring. If you do the research, I think you will find both science and logic back me up.

If you aren't familiar with the term, a "red herring" is not only a kind of fish. It is a literary device used to distract the reader from discovering a truth the writer wants to obscure for the moment. Think of a good mystery, where some evidence comes to light that totally makes you think "the butler did it," when in reality it was the baker or the candlestick maker all along.

In other words, a red herring is used to throw you off the scent of what's really going on in a story. Just imagine a criminal, who, when being chased by tracking dogs, throws a literal red herring as far as he can in one direction and then takes off in the other direction. The dogs go after the fish, and the felon gets away.

So a red herring is a calculated distraction designed to let the bad guy get away with murder. And that's what sexual compatibility is. Because what God wants for your sex life is pretty simple: chastity. That is abstinence outside of marriage and sexual delight in marriage.

But our culture—or more accurately our enemy—throws out the red herring of sexual compatibility to divert our attention away from that goal. The argument goes like this: how can you be certain you will be sexually compatible in marriage if you never experiment sexually with the person you are considering to fill the lifelong role of your monogamous sex partner?

And what an effective red herring sexual compatibility is! Distracting believers who God has called to holiness and luring them into sexual immorality like a dumb dog to a dead fish.

The Only Way to Be Sexually Compatible

Am I saying sexual compatibility is unimportant? Not exactly.

I'm aware that different people have different desires and expectations for sexual frequency, activities, positions, and the like. I get that.

However, after having enjoyed sex for over twenty-eight years with the same person (and only that person), wouldn't you like to know what makes for our "sexual compatibility"?

Believe it or don't, it has almost nothing to do with the sexual desires and expectations we each brought into our marriage. Instead, our sexual compatibility has grown out of (and is nurtured by) our compatibility in other more important areas of our relationship than our sex life.

Let me put it to you this way. You can, if you wish, blow off this little "red herring" lesson, mess around in your dating life, and marry someone who you know ahead of time you really enjoy having sex with.

However, do you know what could very likely happen one or two or ten years later? Your sex life could be boring, stale, or completely dead.

Or you can take my word for it and believe sexual compatibility is just a distraction. Believing this, you might not only marry as a virgin, you might be completely sexually inexperienced (which is actually my earnest prayer for you). Then, after you pledge, "I do," you could find sex awkward, difficult, and even—gasp—disappointing.

However, you know what could happen one or two or ten years later? Your sex life could be amazing, fun, and life-giving to your marriage. Because apart from rare medical or physiological issues, happily married couples generally enjoy happy sex lives. While unhappily married couples usually aren't having much sex at all. At least not with each other.

Compatibility Is *Not* Everything

In the more sophisticated dating apps (i.e., not the swipe-right-for-a-hook-up apps) compatibility is king. In fact, eHarmony, one of the biggest dating apps around, measures twenty-nine different areas of compatibility. You can look that list up online if you like, but in the event that you are actually able to find someone with whom you match up with in twenty-nine different areas of compatibility, I have just two things to say to you:

1. Congratulations on winning the relational lottery.
2. It will be the thirtieth area that's going to kill you.

Again, no couple is compatible in everything. Not even if they are identical twins. In which case they shouldn't be getting married at all.

No, not even if the Supreme Court decides they can.

I don't say that to discourage you from finding out where you are and aren't compatible with the person you're dating but to discourage you from expecting a whole host of compatibilities to guarantee a successful relationship. Because though compatibility can make a relationship easier and more enjoyable, it does not ensure relationship permanence.

The Right Reason to Seek Compatibility

The desire for compatibility can be inspired by many motivations. Here are three common ones, but only one of them is the right motivator.

Selfishness: This motivation says, "I don't want my dating relationship (or future marriage) to be uncomfortable." Sign that selfishness is your motivation: you seek and desire compatibility in areas that make the relationship easier and more enjoyable for you. In fact, this motivation will have a checklist feel to it, where every box begins with "I like …"

- I like football and they like football.
- I like riding bikes and they like riding bikes.
- I like tacos and they like tacos.
- I like to kiss and they like to kiss.
- I like what I like and they like what I like.

Fear: This motivation says, "I don't want my dating relationship (or future marriage) to be unsuccessful." Sign that fear is your motivation: you seek and desire compatibility in *everything.*

Of course, no one wants their dating relationship to be unsuccessful, but success can't be guaranteed in any dating relationship. In other words, success is outside your ability to secure, but being responsible about who you date, when you start dating them, and how you carry out your dating relationship are choices you get to make. Which leads us to the right reason to seek compatibility.

Wisdom: This motivation says, "I don't want my dating relationship (or future marriage) to be irresponsible." Sign that wisdom is your motivation: you seek and require compatibility in areas that spring out of your core identity and convictions.

Compatibility Is Not About Sameness

Important note: You aren't looking for a carbon copy of yourself. You're looking for an effective counterpart to yourself. You don't want a relationship in which you mirror each other, but one in which you complement and mature one another.

For perspective, look to other relationships where compatibility is important: an effective team, a successful company, or a thriving church. Then look for a dating partner with whom your compatibility serves a higher purpose.

The Limits of Compatibility

If compatibility is what holds your relationship together, then what happens when incompatibilities surface over time? Because they will. Trust me!

As the years have passed, Julie and I continually learn new things about each other. And some of those things have revealed incompatibilities we could have never seen until we learned those things.

Likewise, if compatibility is what holds your relationship together, what happens when someone changes? Because you will! We all do.

In some ways, Julie is the same girl I married in college, but in many ways, she is nothing like that college girl. She has matured, developed, mellowed, and toughened in ways I could have never foreseen.

So, though I would still affirm today that Julie and I are well matched, I can also attest that we work well together less because of our "perfect compatibility" and more because we serve a higher purpose than marital satisfaction.

In light of that reality, my prayer is that you will know and serve and delight in a higher purpose than your own personal satisfaction right now as you read the final words of this chapter. And in doing so, you will be preparing for a life-giving, lifelong marriage.

CHAPTER 20:

CALLING, CHEMISTRY, AND COMMITMENT

Some believe that a healthy dating relationship should steadily progress in both emotional/relational intimacy and physical/sexual intimacy. As much sense as that may seem to make, here are four reasons the pursuit of the physical so often overwhelms and derails the pursuit of relational intimacy.

PERCEPTION OF CONTROL

Sex is a conversation. But not just any conversation. The kind of conversation where one thing leads to another, to the point where your passions seem to completely take over, and you are powerless to stop it. And you don't want to, because it feels so good.

In contrast, verbal dialogue is not so frantic. It can meander and spiderweb and ebb and flow. It can progress as rapidly as sex, but if your passions take over in a verbal conversation, it is usually in expression of anger, not pursuit of pleasure. And no one feels good about that.

CALLING, CHEMISTRY, AND COMMITMENT

INTENSITY OF PLEASURE

Physical intimacy activates the pleasure center of the brain in such a powerful way, it even beats video games. Growing a friendship is fun but not quite that fun.

EXPERIENCE OF CONNECTION

Sex can make you feel special, accepted, and loved in the moment, and then create a false sense of closeness. (Remember the Frisky Kittens.) Talking with someone you enjoy being with can make you feel special, accepted, and loved too, but perhaps not to the same intensity. (Remember the Conscientious Cats.)

MENTAL ENGAGEMENT

The frontal cortex of the brain (the part of the brain responsible for higher reasoning, decision-making, morality, and personality) has only one role in sex: self-control. In other words, following your sexual impulses requires very little thought, while resisting your sexual impulses requires a lot.

In contrast, not talking takes very little thought, while choosing to engage in verbal intercourse engages the frontal cortex on a high level as you listen, analyze the information you are receiving, and consider and articulate your responses.

In short, sexual intercourse is the path of least resistance, whereas participating in healthy verbal intercourse is the path of intentional growth.

Ready for some intentional growth right now? Here are our final three DTP Talks.

DTP TALK #8: CALLING

Ever heard a married couple say, "We just grew apart?" That is a couple who lacked a shared calling on their lives which, far more than simply keeping them from growing apart, would have powerfully grown them together.

At FMU, we hold marriage in high esteem; we even consider marriage an awesome calling. But it's not the ultimate calling. Not by a long shot.

So how can you make sure you don't wind up in a marriage with no shared calling?

First, you need to know something about God's calling on your own life. Then you need to discern whether the person you're dating knows something about God's call on their life. Next you need to explore how your respective callings could not only compliment but enhance the potential of your individual callings.

What Is a Calling?

Our culture doesn't encourage us to pursue a calling as much as it encourages us to chase our dreams. And the two are not the same thing.

- A dream comes from your *heart*, but a calling comes from your *God*.

- A dream is about becoming who you *want* to be, but a calling is about becoming who you *were made* to be.

- A dream is about what *you* want for your life, but a calling is about what *God* wants for your life.

- A dream is driven by *passion*, but a calling is driven by *purpose*.

- A dream begins (and *usually* ends) with *you*, but a calling begins (and *always* ends) with *God*.

- A dream is often rooted in *fantasy* (what you hope will happen in your future), but a calling is always rooted in *reality* (what God will make happen in your future).

- A dream *drives* you to live in the *hoped-for future*, but a calling *empowers* you to live in the *God-ordained present*.

- A dream usually has you *grasping for the power* necessary to make it happen, while a calling always has you *gripped by the peace* found in God's sovereignty.

Can you see what an important thing a sense of calling is? Even unbelievers thrive better when pursuing what they believe to be a calling. Instead of God, that calling might come from their parents, or their country, or the universe, or the wise Yoda in their life (whoever that may be). Or the force, for that matter.

Can you see how important a shared sense of calling would be in your future marriage?

Marriage Is *Not* the Mission

Julie and I DON'T have the marriage we do simply because we enjoy common interests, have our identity firmly grounded in Christ, share values and convictions, and are compatible.

All of those things are important. That's why they comprise five of our DTP talks, but Julie and I aren't merely *married* to each other. We are on a *mission* together. And not just because we run a ministry now.

Even before FMU was a thing, Julie and I have chased after God's call on our lives together. That calling has almost always had us serving in the youth ministry of whatever church we were at. It's had us opening our home to share food, fellowship, Bible study, and prayer with family and friends. And for all but the first two years of our marriage, our calling has included one of the most fearful missions in life: parenting.

You may never start a ministry together with your future spouse. You may never be able to have kids. Regardless, God has a call on your life—probably more than one as you grow and mature and age together. And God will have a call on your marriage—probably more than one.

That said, if you make marriage your mission in life, it's going to disappoint, because while marriage is a truly awesome calling, God calls believers into marriage in order to impact their world for His kingdom purposes. In other words, marriage isn't an end, but a means to an end: probably several ends.

How Can You Tell If Your Date Has a Sense of Calling?

To discover if the person you're dating has a sense of calling, try asking one or more questions like these:

- How have you seen God use your faith
  (or passions, knowledge, skills, or strengths)?

- Is there something you hope God will do through you in
  this season of life, or by the time you [insert milestone here]
  (or before you die)?

- What gets you up in the morning? What keeps you going
  through the day? What keeps you up at night?

- What difference for the kingdom do you feel you're *supposed* to make?

To be certain, if you asked one or more of those questions and got a passionate response full of conviction, that would tell you a lot about the maturity of the person you're dating and their readiness for whatever the future held, whether that included marriage to you or not.

It would also tell you much about how compatible you would be together. For instance, if you see obvious synergy between how God's leading you and how they see God leading them, that would be a meaningful indicator of your marriage potential together.

In contrast, if you feel indifferent or conflicted when they talk about what they sense God's will is for their life, that should be a huge red flag that regardless of how passionate they may be, they probably aren't the right person for you.

Many faithful followers of Jesus don't necessarily feel comfortable discussing life on an ontological level like this. That's no crime. So instead of the direct-question approach, you can look for the evidence of calling in your date by observing how they talk and act.

- Since a calling comes from your God, not your heart, **observe how much your date talks about God's will and wanting to know it.**

- Since a calling is about becoming who you were made to be, not necessarily who you want to be, **observe whether your date seems teachable or humble.**

- Since a calling is about what God wants for your life, not what you want, **observe how flexible your date is.**

- Since a calling is driven by purpose, not just passion, **observe whether your date seems to chase various (even conflicting) passions or if their passions seem aligned in a specific direction.**

- Since a calling begins and ends with God, not yourself, **observe whether your date lives to serve others or themselves.**

- Since a calling is always rooted in reality, not fantasy, **observe whether your date has a realistic or overinflated appraisal of their gifts and potential.**

- Since a calling empowers you to live in the God-ordained present, not your hoped-for future, **observe whether your date seems content and present in the moment or restless, anxious, or constantly distracted.**

- Since a calling comes with God's peace that passes understanding, **observe how your date handles conflict, disappointment, and challenges.**

A Calling Is *Not* an Obligation

Ever known a miserable married couple who have given up on making their marriage work, yet they won't divorce? They promised "until death" and they meant it, so they're going to "stick it out" until one of them dies. Indeed, they'd be more likely to actually kill each other than divorce.

That is a couple who views the call of marriage as an obligation instead of an honor.

"I'm keeping my vows," they will defiantly declare. Like a soldier following the orders of a commanding officer, they don't have to like it. They must simply honor the chain of command.

Is that all marriage vows are about? Not divorcing? Hanging on until death? No! It's not! While "until death" is a critical piece of the traditional vows, it's the *context* of the vows. Not the actual *content*.

The marriage vows aren't so much about what you're committing *not* to do, but about what you are committing you *will* do: namely proactively and sacrificially love, honor, and cherish each other. And for how long? This is where the "until death do us part" comes in.

So, if you want a marriage where you both honor your marriage vows out of honor instead of obligation, then you want to find the sort of partner who already sees God's calling in other areas of their life as an honor and not an obligation.

Do you see how significant a sense of calling is? And how important it is to view God's calling on your life, in every season, not as an obligation, but an honor?

DTP TALK #9: CHEMISTRY

If you aren't crazy about someone you've been dating for a couple months, that's a good sign they're probably not right for you. All the more so if they've clearly declared their deep and abiding romantic interest in you, while you're like "Meh," or worse, "Ew!"

At the very least it would indicate the time is not right to move forward with a dating relationship. I know you don't want to break their heart, but you also want to embrace the truth. And the truth is, no healthy human being wants to be in a dating relationship where their partner isn't as emotionally invested as they are.

This reality goes both ways, so if you aren't sure how someone feels about you after a couple months of dating, you can safely assume they're not that into you. All the more so if you've made your passions impossible to miss.

Perhaps they'll wake up someday and realize you are the cat's meow. But believe it or not, they're more likely to realize that after you've backed away from a dating relationship and they've had a chance to experience life without your constant attention, than they are if you're continually at their feet like a dog begging for table scraps of their love.

Why We Worship Chemistry

The sequence of the DTP talks in this chapter is not necessarily in order of importance. Even still, there's a reason chemistry didn't even make the Top 5, while chemistry often seems to be #1 on everyone else's list of things to confirm in a dating relationship.

Why do we seem to literally worship chemistry? The most obvious reason: it's the one characteristic unique to a dating relationship.

Great relationships of all sorts and sizes are characterized by sharing common interests, core identity, values, convictions, compatibility, and calling, while at the same time *not* sharing romantic interest.

So it's easy to see how this unique characteristic becomes the only one that receives significant consideration as people date.

Moreover, sharing romantic chemistry makes sharing common interests or values seem boring. Chemistry is fun, exciting, and addictive. And I mean that last adjective literally, because they don't call it "chemistry" for nothing.

The Actual Chemistry Behind Sharing Chemistry

The feelings of romance are caused by neurochemistry lighting up your brain in ways that can be highly addictive.

How would one define the chemistry of love? If you had to pick, which of the following would you compare to that feeling of being madly in love:

- **Cocaine**: a stimulant that makes you feel more energetic and confident

- **Marijuana**: a depressant that makes you feel relaxed and chill

- **LSD**: a hallucinogen that distorts your perception of reality

The correct answer? ALL OF THEM! Indeed, the brain chemistry of being in love delivers:

- **Dopamine**—Makes you excited every time you think of your love or just get a text from them and keeps you continually obsessed with the thought of when you'll see them again.

- **Norepinephrine**—Gives you that "head over heels" feeling every time you're around your love or even see their picture.

- **Phenylethylamine**—Hits you like meth, but the dealer is your significant other. And the drug itself is your significant other.

- **Serotonin**—Delivers that relaxed and blissful disposition when you're staring into the eyes of your love or just daydreaming about staring into their eyes.

- **Oxytocin**—Stimulated by physical touch, this so-called "cuddle drug" not only makes you feel safe and calm but mysteriously bonded to your love.

Can you see why something responsible for such brain chemistry could not only become addictive but something we're sorely tempted to worship?

Chemistry Can Connect You, but It Cannot Keep You

To help us understand the danger of depending on romantic chemistry in relationships, it might help to consider other types of chemistry.

Organic chemistry explains how a diamond is formed when intense underground pressure transforms common carbon into a rare diamond. It also explains how underground pressure causes a volcanic eruption. Likewise in relationships, romantic chemistry can result in relationships as tough and beautiful as a diamond or as tragic and destructive as a volcano.

Nuclear chemistry allows us to power cities or completely destroy them. Similarly, romantic chemistry can energize the early stages of a relationship, only to lead to that relationship's inevitable destruction.

DATE LIKE YOU KNOW WHAT YOU'RE DOING

Which leads us to an essential truth to understand: though romantic chemistry often brings people together and even bonds them—often powerfully—the chemistry of romantic attraction is not permanent. Which is to say, chemistry can connect you, but it cannot keep you.

In spite of this reality, millions of starry-eyed, star-crossed lovers will marry, believing the undeniable connection created by the mutual chemistry they share is irrefutable evidence that their relationship will stand the test of time. Their feelings are real, but they're not necessarily right.

So if chemistry can't keep you, what can? That's the topic of our last DTP talk.

DTP TALK #10: COMMITMENT

Regardless of the role chemistry plays in your relationship with your future spouse—and it *must* play some role—you want to make sure the person you're dating possesses the key characteristic necessary to maintain a life-giving, lifelong marriage. And that would be commitment.

Commitment—not chemistry—is what holds any relationship together. A band that lacks commitment eventually breaks up, no matter how undeniable their chemistry on stage. A team that lacks commitment eventually falls apart, no matter how effective their chemistry on the field. And a couple that lacks commitment eventually calls it quits, no matter how adorable their chemistry when they're together.

Afraid of Commitment?

If you haven't heard it from someone dating in real life, you've heard it in the movies: "I'm afraid of commitment."

It's the perfect explanation for someone who's wanting to back out of a developing relationship. They pull the "commitment" card.

It's supposed to be a kind way to communicate, "It's not you. It's me." In truth, it's either cowardly or childish. Or both.

If it is just an excuse, as it usually is, then be honest and share the real reason you don't feel comfortable moving forward in the relationship. If you don't know the real reason, then seek wise counsel from someone who knows and loves you well and knows and loves God well.

However, if you truly are afraid of commitment in general, you have no business dating because, as we've already said, commitment is what holds any healthy relationship together. Further, a committed relationship is precisely what any two healthy daters are hoping for.

It's no crime not to be interested in a committed dating relationship or even to be afraid of it. Perhaps you ought to be afraid of a committed dating relationship right now. Not that you aren't worthy of one but that you're just not ready yet.

And if you're realizing this is true while you're already in a dating relationship, then come clean. Don't just say, "I'm afraid of commitment," or even, "I'm not ready for a serious dating relationship right now," but admit, "I was wrong to even start this dating relationship. I'm sorry for the hurt this may cause you. You deserve a person who's ready to move forward, and that person is not me."

Things like that are hard to say, but a true confession will go a long way toward righting your wrong and giving the other person the closure they need to move forward without you.

Why Cohabitation Doesn't Prepare You for Marriage

As you know, the point of the marriage ceremony is exchanging the marriage vows, and the point of the marriage vows is entering the marriage covenant, and the marriage covenant is basically the commitment of all human commitments.

Subsequently, the marriage covenant is the defining characteristic of a healthy, vibrant marriage. Indeed, all the benefits of marriage are supposed to be the fruit of the lifetime commitment on the part of both individuals to love, honor, and cherish one another.

But what's the point of cohabitation? If we're honest, the whole reason someone would choose to cohabit instead of marry is because they expressly *don't* want to commit for life. At least not yet. Maybe in the future, yes, but for now they want "an out."

Some just want to play house. Many see the benefit of having a roommate (with benefits). But even in those situations where the couple is seriously wanting to move toward marriage, it's still not about committing. It's about testing the relationship to see if the relationship should lead to marriage.

While this way of "testing" a relationship ahead of marriage may now be considered the norm—and it *is* (70% of couples now cohabit ahead of marriage)—it's still *not* about commitment.[10]

Sure you can commit to cohabiting long-term, but you can't compare a "*long-term* commitment" to a *lifetime* commitment. And, frankly, compared to a lifetime commitment, even a five-year commitment is *not* a long-term commitment.

So what if you get along fabulously cohabiting for six months or even six years? Many married couples do the same. Six months simply can't tell you how well you'll get along after six years, and six years can't tell you how well you'll get along for the rest of your life.

To be clear, marriage is not about testing a relationship but about testing yourself. It's about finding out what you're really made of and who you

---

[10] Lyman Stone and Brad Wilcox, *"Research: Religious Americans Less Likely to Divorce,"* ChristianityToday.com (Christianity Today, December 14, 2021), https://www.christianitytoday.com/ct/2021/december-web-only/marriage-divorce-cohabitation-religious-americans-study.html.

really want to be. It's not about "trying out" a relationship but about a relationship "trying you," refining you, maturing you, and strengthening you.

What Courtship and Cohabitation Have in Common

Starting in the 1990s, many (but not all) in the courtship movement determined they would wait until they believed they should marry someone before they dated them, so they more or less made the marriage commitment up front.

A lot of pressure for that first cup of coffee, right? Do you shop for rings on the second date? Or play it safe, and wait for the third? Or do the parents pick out the rings?

Curiously, couples who hold off on that first date until they're convinced they have found the person they will marry have much in common with couples who wait to cohabit until they think they're going to get married. Because couples in both categories are trying to predict something they really can't, and in doing so, they presume upon the future. They're assuming they'll eventually marry, without actually committing to do so. And in their presumption, they often act "committed" or "married" in ways they shouldn't (whether those acts involve shopping for rings or jumping in the sack prematurely).

How Can You Know If They Will Commit?

Instead of wondering if the person you're dating can commit, note if they already *do* commit. Don't try to predict their future behavior. Simply pay attention to their behavior in the present. Carefully observe over time how the person you're into is "into" their current commitments. Consider the following areas:

- **Family**—How do they *talk* about their family (disrespectfully or honorably, ungratefully or appreciatively)? How do they *treat* their family (dismissively or attentively, rudely or respectfully)? How do they *prioritize* their family? Do they spend time with them or avoid them? Do they care for them or dismiss them? Do they make sacrifices for them or do they sacrifice their family for other things or other people? Or you?

- **Friends**—Same questions as above, plus these questions: Do they have friends they've known for years? Do they have close friends?

- **Church**—Are they church-hoppers, church-shoppers, or church-samplers? Or are they faithfully attending, giving, serving, and connecting?

- **Studies**—Do they treat their studies like an obligation or a calling? Do they seek to excel or just get by?

- **Job**—Do they move up in the ranks wherever they work, or do they more or less move from job to job? Are they committed to excellence, personal growth, and their career future or are they just in it for the paycheck?

Someone who can't or won't show commitment in any of those areas shouldn't be expected to stand faithful and true in the life-long covenant of marriage. They may very well be a fine human being made in the image of God, but they are not ready for a dating commitment.

Conversely, someone who shows a pattern of commitment across multiple areas of their life demonstrates the kind of character necessary for thriving in the marriage covenant. That's no guarantee, of course, but it sure beats trying to guess the future.

DON'T TREAT DATING LIKE A JOB INTERVIEW

Covering all these subjects might seem overwhelming, but remember you're trying to build a friendship and that should be fun!

Don't treat dating like a job interview. All of this shouldn't feel like work. It should feel like an adventure! It shouldn't feel like a list of chores, but a process of discovery.

Don't get obsessed with whether this person will turn out to be "the one." Keep your head in the game, meaning in the moment in which you find yourself.

Final quick tips as you attempt to learn and share this information:

1. Take your time—REMEMBER: love is first and foremost what?

2. Be honest—If they don't like the real you, you need to move on.

3. Have fun—If you can't shake the stress or sense of obligation, seek wise counsel!

This chapter marks the end of the seventh lesson in an 8-week LoveEd study. For discussion questions and resources go to:

FMUniversity.net/DatePrep-wk7

CHAPTER 21:

WHAT EVERYONE SHOULD KNOW ABOUT MARRIAGE BEFORE THEY EVER DATE

Our mission at FMU is to empower students and young adults to grow spiritually and date wisely so they can marry well!

Desiring that for you, we've talked all about wise dating, as well as the importance of spiritual growth to your dating adventure. In doing so, we've focused on the purpose of your dating life, but now it's time to talk about the goal of your dating life.

> **Friends-First Dating:** Intentional time invested in one other person for the purpose of growing a friendship that might lead to **a life-giving, lifelong marriage.**

Note: with friends-first dating, the goal isn't merely marriage. It's a life-giving, lifelong marriage. One that blesses the world as much as it blesses the two of you.

If that sounds like the kind of marriage you'd like for yourself, we at FMU want to help you reach that goal. In fact, we'd like to empower you to prepare for your future marriage like you would a successful career: intentionally, intelligently, and in advance.

SHOULD YOU REALLY BE THINKING ABOUT MARRIAGE NOW?

You may be wondering if it's too early to seriously turn your attention to the aspiration of marriage. Maybe you have more school ahead of you, or career goals, or other bucket-list items.

Even the adults in your life may be urging you to focus on other priorities, perhaps *anything* other than marriage.

Maybe they're right. Or maybe, when we "think about marriage," there's a difference between *longing* for marriage and *preparing* for marriage. When some confess to "thinking about marriage all the time," they likely mean they long for it. But when I refer to "thinking about marriage," I'm talking about preparing for it.

Should you be *longing* for marriage? That depends on your age, maturity level, and relationship status.

Should you be *preparing* for marriage? That depends on whether you believe you're called to marriage.

If you believe you are, then it's never too early to prepare. Especially if you want to date. Or already are dating. In other words, if you're currently dating, you should be preparing for the goal you hope your dating life will lead to.

But even if you aren't seriously dating now, remember Paul's injunction from 1 Corinthians 7. If your sex drive indicates you are likely made for marriage, then as you endeavor to *control* your sex drive, why not at the same time prepare for the relationship which will enable you to *enjoy* your sex drive?

However, before we consider what that preparation might look like, we first need to address one key word in our definition of friends-first dating.

I'm talking about the word that lies between our stated purpose and goal—namely the word "might." As in, "growing a friendship that **might** lead to a life-giving, lifelong marriage."

GOD DOES NOT PROMISE MARRIAGE

I cannot promise what our God does not. Therefore, friends-first dating doesn't say that intentional time invested in one other person for the purpose of growing a friendship *will* lead to a life-giving, lifelong marriage. It only says it *might*. And "might" means "might." It means risk. But isn't this true in any life endeavor, no matter how wisely you approach it?

Consider our analogy in Chapter 1 where we compared dating to learning how to drive a car. You can follow all the rules of the road, exercising great care with constant alertness, and still wind up in an accident.

Does this reality mean we just say, "Whatever," and drive with reckless abandon? Of course not. Instead, being aware of all that is out of our control should compel us to do all that is within our control, inspiring us to drive more carefully and alertly.

In the same way, you could make all the right dating decisions (if that were possible) and still end up experiencing heartbreak, rejection, and regret. You could end up in a miserable marriage. You could even end up divorced. But let this sober reality inspire you to date all the more with diligence and devotion to wisdom and grace.

You will never regret walking in wisdom and grace … in the end. And when I say, "in the end," I'm not referring to your wedding day.

The end will not be when you hear your earthly love declare, "I do," but when you hear your First Love say, "Well done!"

Don't you want to hear those words "Well done" even more than you want to hear the words "I do"? Then date accordingly and trust Him! He has

WHAT EVERYONE SHOULD KNOW ABOUT MARRIAGE BEFORE THEY EVER DATE

your best interests at heart, even if your best interests don't wind up including the marriage you hoped for. Or even marriage at all.

WHAT IF YOU NEVER MARRY?

At this point, you might be wondering why you want to think about marriage (much less prepare for marriage) when you don't even know if you'll ever get there. What's the point?

Great question. To which I will respond with another question. Should people stop going to school because their education may fail to secure them the career they hope for?

Hopefully not, because a great education should deliver value to the student as they submit to the process of learning, growing, and changing into a different person. True education is less about preparing to succeed in a specific set of tasks and more about becoming a certain kind of person who can succeed in life in general. In other words, it should be less about knowledge and more about character.

Indeed, the very process of preparing for your career empowers you to focus your sights on the kind of work you were made for. In the same way, the very process of preparing for your future marriage should help you focus your sights on the kind of relationships you were made for. One of those relationships likely being marriage.

That said, there is much you can do to improve your chances of reaching the goal of a life-giving, lifelong marriage, and this is where the preparation comes in.

IMPROVE YOUR CHANCES AT A ROCK STAR MARRIAGE

When it comes to our career, we quickly make the logical connection between preparation and expectation. In other words, the higher our career aspirations, the more time we expect to invest in our education.

We all understand that a four-year college degree will give us more career opportunities than a high school diploma, while a high school graduate will generally enjoy far higher earning potential than a high school drop-out. Indeed, many career fields are completely out of reach unless you are willing to go to grad school. And we're appreciative of this extra required education whenever we need to see a doctor or hire a lawyer. Right?

But what happens when it comes to marriage? All logic goes out the window. There's no education required for marriage, so it's assumed none is needed. And that's another reason why we have divorce.

Sure, many get premarital counseling (and you should), but if that's the sum total of all the time and effort you put into preparing for the demands of your future marriage, you'll likely find it to be too little too late.

Actually, the best premarital programs deliver too *much* too late, as they offer far more knowledge, skills, and tools than mere mortals can reasonably expect to absorb in a handful of classes. Especially love birds with their hearts all atwitter.

Again, if we were to compare marriage to career, premarital counseling would be equivalent to on-the-job training; the education you don't get until the company has already agreed to bring you on.

Yet, if marriage was something you had to apply for like a job, the full job description would be intimidating to say the least. Overwhelming to be more accurate. Would you expect a few hours of on-the-job training to set you up to secure and succeed at a high-level job description?

No? Then why would we treat marriage that way?

So, the one thing everyone should know about marriage before they ever date is simply this: if you expect to enjoy a life-giving, lifelong marriage, you should expect to prepare for it ahead of time. Perhaps you might want something equivalent to a college education.

IF YOU CAN'T MAJOR IN MARRIAGE HOW CAN YOU PREPARE?

If colleges don't offer majors in marriage, how do you go about preparing for your future marriage like you would a successful career?

Why not commit to the same tasks we're encouraged to tackle in preparation for and growth in our careers? For example:

- Read books
- Talk to experts
- Attend classes
- Gain experience

Marriage: Read All About It

You might remember from the introduction that the whole inspiration for writing this book for you was the marriage book my mom gave me when I was in my early 20s, still in college, and not in any dating relationship at all.

I think my mom was onto something, and that one book changed the trajectory of my life. But do you only read one book in high school? What about college? Grad school?

Of course not! So when you're done with this book, keep on reading, my friend. And not just about dating. Read actual marriage books which can help you understand the goal you want your dating life to take you to. Find our recommended reading list at the link at the end of this chapter.

That said, you can read much online without ever buying another book. In fact, we've got a veritable treasure trove of 400+ blog posts on our website (FMUniversity.net), plus over 250 videos!

Seek Out the Advice of Rock Stars

We call "expert" couples who have learned how to rock 30+ years of marriage "rock stars." If they've been married that long and still get a twinkle in their eye when talking about each other, they should prove to be fountains of grace-filled wisdom.

However, if you've never been married at all, a couple married ten years will have more experience than you have. Ask them questions and listen to their answers. Observe how they relate, talk about each other, and prioritize their marriage and family life.

Ultimately, you want to find mentors who are rocking the kind of marriage you would like to rock.

But keep in mind, not all experts are great teachers. Some who know their subject matter like no one else, simply can't adequately explain what comes so naturally to them.

I realized this the hard way when interviewing a couple at our church who had been married for 60+ years. I spent an hour with them, trying to find out how they stayed so happy together for so long, but their best—actually only—go-to advice?

> "Divorce was just never on the table for us.
> Murder? Yes. But divorce? No!"

That was funny and all, but it doesn't give you much to go on, does it? That's why you want to learn from great teachers too! Of course, you can learn from their books, but deeper learning often happens in the classroom setting.

Why Single People Should Attend Marriage Conferences

Of course, every single marriage conference and seminar is marketed to (and will be filled with) engaged and married couples, so if you were to attend one as a single person, it's likely to feel awkward at first.

Until you explain to the first married couple you meet that you're coming so you can prepare for marriage in advance. Then you may watch tears well up in their eyes as they look at one another and say, "Why didn't *we* think of that?!"

And then they might get out their phones and start texting eligible singles they have been praying for at their church, "We're at a conference trying to strengthen our marriage, but YOU should get your butt down here now, so you can plan ahead … Plus there's someone we want you to meet."

Hey, it could happen!

You may want to skip the session on sex, since they'd be presenting the material to those who could conceivably implement it that very night. (Which shouldn't be you.) Then again, they'll likely share truth that could empower you to view marital sex rightly and inspire you to deal with your sexual past before marriage. Ask the seminar director for their advice.

All of this sound too edgy? Are you an introvert? Are you not yet in your 20s? Then you can go through a video curriculum.

Regardless, if you want to prepare for your future marriage like a successful career, you ought to consider attending a couple classes.

The Experience You Need for Marriage

What kind of experience can prepare you for marriage? We've talked a lot about that throughout the pages of this book.

- Determine to heal from your past. Get counseling if needed.

- Learn how to identify, declare, and deal with your issues. Not everything is your parents' fault.

- Commit to a church body where you are giving and growing.

- Grow deep friendships. Learn to share honestly with and pray faithfully for your closest friends.

- Seek out and submit to mentors who you learn from and are accountable to.

- Date like a boss: like you want to leave every person you ever date a better person for having gone out with you.

Bottom line, learn to make your life about relationships, first and foremost with the God who asked me to write this book for you, and then in every area of life.

- Learn to love unconditionally. Even the unlovable people in your life. Especially the unlovable people in your life. Even if that means just praying for them from afar.

- Learn to serve sacrificially. Not as a martyr or victim, but as a servant of Christ!

- Learn to witness faithfully in each and every situation.

DATE WITH THE END IN MIND

I'll never forget when I asked Julie to be my girlfriend, lip-syncing "This is the Way Love Is" by the 77s. (Yes, there was lip-synching before TikTok.) I'll never forget sharing my first ice cream sundae with her. The first ice cream sundae I had *ever* shared with *any* girl.

I'll never forget the first time I told Julie I loved her, sitting with her in the band tower in the middle of the intramural fields under a starry sky. And I'll never forget her reaction.

I knew the words "I love you" were not carelessly spoken by her, so when I decided to reveal my feelings, I didn't expect her to respond in kind.

I anticipated that she would need more time before feeling confident in confessing her affections. I didn't want to manipulate her into revealing feelings she wasn't ready to share. And, honestly, I didn't think I *could* manipulate her into doing so. (The force was strong with her.) But even today, recalling her response makes my skin tingle.

"I've known that I love you for some time."

Right out of a movie, right?

However, while our dating life was truly delightful, our married life has proven to be deeply meaningful. While our engagement was a time of excitement and anticipation, our marriage has been a profound life experience.

Odds are, it will be for you too! Especially if you're dating with the end in mind. Not obsessed with the goal of marriage, but focused on the purpose of growing the kind of friendship more likely to lead you to your goal.

DON'T SAY "I LOVE YOU" TOO SOON

I'm so glad I waited to tell Julie I loved her. Because once you cross that threshold, there's no going back to the way things were. Either your relationship takes a turn for the worse and soul ties are severed, leaving heartbreak, rejection, and regret. Or you continue toward marriage—for better or for worse.

Not for better and better. For better or for worse.

When you say, "I love you," you have to do so knowing the worse *will* come. Days when the lovey dovey affection of young love will *not* sustain you. Only sacrificial commitment.

Many other words Julie and I have shared over the course of our marriage have drawn us closer than we could have imagined back when we first said "I love you" under the stars. Even though many of those words came not out of joy but disappointment and even great loss as our lives seemed to be falling apart:

"I do."

"Let's move to Oregon!"

"It's a boy!"

"Let's move to Portland!"

"The doctor says I have appendicitis, and they have to operate right away."

"It's a girl!"

"My mom killed herself."

"The realtor says they accepted our offer! We're going to own our first home!"

"I'm pregnant again!"

"I lost my job."

That job loss happened only three months after we bought that first home and were pregnant with our third child. And all the words above were shared within the first seven years of our marriage.

All of that to say, you have no idea what lies ahead of you! So draw nearer and nearer to the God who does! And don't say, "I love you," too soon.

MY FINAL BLESSING

I wish you God's richest blessings in every one of your relationships. That's why I wrote this book for you. It's only a guide, but I pray it empowers you to grow spiritually and date wisely so you can marry well. And if it does, be sure to send us a wedding invite! Better yet, drop us a note after your ten-year anniversary.

Until then, consider this my prayer for you in your dating life:

For God is my witness, how I yearn for you all with the affection of Christ Jesus. And it is my prayer that your love may abound more and more, with knowledge and all discernment, so that you may approve what is excellent, and so be pure and blameless for the day of Christ, filled with the fruit of righteousness that comes through Jesus Christ, to the glory and praise of God. —Philippians 1:8-11 ESV

This chapter marks the end
of the final lesson in an 8-week
LoveEd study. For discussion questions
and resources go to:

FMUniversity.net/DatePrep-wk8

ACKNOWLEDGMENTS

First, I must thank the God who put the fire in my soul not only to write this book, but also to pursue the call of empowering students and young adults to grow spiritually and date wisely so they can marry well.

Secondly, I am grateful for Julie, my amazing, beautiful, creative, deep-thinking, energetic, faithful, garden-growing, hopeful, inspiring, Jesus-following, keen, lifelong-learning, maverick, never-giving-up-never-surrendering, out-of-the-box-thinking, prayer-warring, quick-witted, running-for-the-prize, sweet-and-sassy, tested-and-true, understanding, virtuous, wise, xenodo-chial, youthful, and zealous-for-the-word wife. Thank you for being my best friend, my bride, my co-pilot in parenting, and my partner in ministry!

Thirdly, I have to thank my mom who planted the seed for this book and my dad who watered it.

A huge thank you to our FMU board members—from David, Hillary, Michael, and Stefani who were with us from the start, to Charlie, Anna, Callum, Kate, and Julieann who were there to see the launch of this book. Your belief in our mission and commitment to the call is an inspiration to Julie and me. How could we have persevered to this point without you?

Thanks to all the students and young adults who over the course of 19+ years of teaching and discipling have been (more or less) guinea pigs in the development of the content of this book.

I'm also incredibly grateful to Dr. Mark Coppenger, Gary Thomas, Dr. John Van Epp, Bob Lepine, Dr. Joe McIlhaney, Lisa Anderson, Dr. Joe Malone, and Ami Sauer for their willingness to read the rough draft of this book, not for themselves, but to lend their personal endorsements to help get this book in the hands of those it might bless. (So I guess they read it for *you*.)

Lastly, but not leastly, thanks to my publishing team, beginning with my trusty editors, Lori Lynn and Mary Rembert. In addition to catching the spelling, grammar, and punctuation mistakes I can't see, they made me do things like rewrite both the intro and the closing of this book, as well as cut about 25% of the original content, so that it wouldn't be the size of *War & Peace*. (Yes, you, the reader owe them MUCH thanks.) Also thankful to Jesse Gibbs and all the publishing party people at BookBaby.

ABOUT THE AUTHOR

Michael Johnson is the President and Dean of Dating at Future Marriage University (FMU), a 501(c)(3) non-profit ministry co-founded with his wife, Julie.

The mission of FMU is to empower students and young adults to grow spiritually and date wisely so they can marry well. To accomplish this, FMU offers love education (LoveEd for short) through classes, blog posts, videos, social media, and speaking engagements (and now this book). Michael has a blast sharing practical, Biblical truth on sex, dating, and relationships, to inspire and lead the wise individual to prepare for their future marriage like a successful career: intentionally, intelligently, and in advance.

The first thing Michael ever wrote was "My Darling's Moving From Missouri," a stirring love song he penned when he was only nine and didn't even have a "darling." And he never got one until college, but that turned out to be for the best, both for Michael and all those other potential "darling" girlfriends. Michael and Julie have known marital bliss since 1993, raised five children together since 1995, and lived in the Nashville area since 2001.

For more LoveEd resources, booking inquiries, or info about FMU, check out their website:

FMUniversity.net